ToMorgan Patterson

3.00

LIBRARY ROOM
CINCINNATI BAPTIST BIBLE COLLEGE
CINCINNATI, OHIO

CONSCIENCE AND COMPROMISE

LIBRARY ROOM
CINCINNATI BAPTIST BIBLE COLLEGE
CINCINNATI, OHIO

Books by
EDWARD LEROY LONG, JR.
Published by the Westminster Press

Conscience and Compromise:
An Outline of Protestant Casuistry

Religious Beliefs of American Scientists

The Christian Response to the Atomic Crisis

CONSCIENCE
AND
COMPROMISE

An Approach to Protestant Casuistry

EDWARD LEROY LONG, JR.

LIBRARY ROOM
CINCINNATI BAPTIST BIBLE COLLEGE
CINCINNATI, OHIO

Philadelphia

THE WESTMINSTER PRESS

COPYRIGHT, MCMLIV, BY WALTER L. JENKINS

All rights reserved — no part of this book may be reproduced in any form without permission in writing from the publisher, except by a reviewer who wishes to quote brief passages in connection with a review in magazine or newspaper.

Library of Congress Catalog Card Number: 54–5280

PRINTED IN THE UNITED STATES OF AMERICA

LIBRARY ROOM
CINCINNATI BAPTIST BIBLE COLLEGE
CINCINNATI, OHIO

Contents

Foreword

CHRISTIANS in all ages have had to be concerned about the relationship of their religious faith to the daily moral decisions that they make as members of society at large. The burden of this concern rests no more lightly upon Christians of this generation than it has upon those of previous generations — rather, it rests more heavily. The Church today lives in a secular culture, which not only fails to live by Christian standards (as have all cultures), but even rejects and scorns these standards in subtle hostility and open ridicule. Not since the Church was persecuted by the Roman Empire have the forces in culture seeking to destroy the distinctive moral witness of Christians been so strong as they are in this generation. The situation is the more serious today because few people recognize the contrast between the secularized standards of our age and the moral principles of Christianity. In America particularly, both those in the Church and those outside its fold harbor the vague illusion that our common life is " Christian."

There is much in American life that Christians, in common with all citizens, will cherish and support. The democratic tradition of the West, in which our land plays a distinctive role, has managed to secure the blessings of liberty and to accompany them with a high degree of legal, and a proximate degree of economic, justice for great numbers of our people.

As compared to any alternative, particularly that of contemporary Communism, the democratic nation is beyond doubt the most conducive situation for the exercise of Christian morality. Even so, as seen from the ultimate perspective of faith, its secular culture must be judged apostate. Its effect upon the Christian conscience presents that conscience with choices involving less than full expressions of Christian love.

The problem of compromise is a perennial one for the Christian who must live in a secular world. He must live amid harsh realities in which choices are always difficult and only inadequate applications of Christian love are possible. Compromise in this agonized sense means the making of imperfect choices in situations where no perfect choices exist. In one sense this is not compromise — it is not the disloyal abandonment of Christian standards for the sake of self. But it is compromise in the constructive sense, the action of those trying to serve God in difficult places.

Compromise in the destructive sense, consisting of disloyalty to Christ and utter abandon to the standards of the world, is apostasy and must be avoided by the man of faith. This book argues strongly for the necessity of compromise in the agonized sense and equally strongly against compromise in the apostate sense.

Speaking of the relation of the Christian to the world about him, W. Norman Pittenger has observed:

"To become a Christian is not to be given a simple solution of one's difficulties. It is, in certain ways, to be given even more problems that must be solved. . . . [The Christian] still has the problems; and he must still live in a secular environment. If he fails to come to some kind of terms with that environment, he will simply destroy himself. If he accepts it completely, he will deny his Christian profession. Hence he must try to compromise.

"Both the word and the idea of 'compromise' are very much disliked by many of our contemporary religious writers. Yet in some degree everyone does compromise; if life is to be a possibility at all, one must do so. The real danger in compromise comes if and when it is indulged in without understanding and without principle. Now in the process of adjustment to the world and its ways, the Christian must know what he is about; one of the real contributions the 'cell' [or group of convinced and dedicated Christians] can make to him personally is that it can keep him alive to his compromising, and give him the strength to maintain his firm Christian position and point of view, at the very time he is involved in secular assumptions that are not his own and is accepting by necessity a social situation that he believes imperfect. Further, the Christian Church itself through its theologians and moralists can be of enormous help to the practicing Christian in this connection. It can work out, for this time and for tomorrow, what we may flatly describe as a 'casuistry' by which life will be possible for the ordinary Christian man or woman" (*The Historic Faith and a Changing World,* pp. 171 f. Oxford University Press, 1950).

The fundamental meaning of the word " casuistry " refers to the process of relating the high demands of faith to the perplexing moral dilemmas that appear in daily life. With this fundamental process all Christians are concerned, and it receives the primary consideration in this book. In the history of the Church, however, the word " casuistry " has been applied not only to the process of guiding conscience, which is the task that Dr. Pittenger assigns it, but to the confessional process by which penitents have been assessed penalties through the performance of which they could earn their pardon. Protestantism, stressing as it does the place of faith in the justification of the sinner, will be wary of casuistry in this penitential sense. Even so, the minister who counsels troubled parishioners ought to bring the implications of justification by faith into meaningful relationship to the concrete guilts that vex men's souls. It is only in the work of the parish minister that both these functions of casuistry can come to fruition. Upon the shepherds of Christian flocks falls the difficult though glorious task of translating the implications of faith into terms relevant to the local and changing problems of their people.

A book cannot give guidance for every type of case, but it can help to acquaint those who read it with the general character of the problem of relating faith to life. It can outline the nature of casuistry needed to deal with the problem. Any person will be better able to translate casuistry into practical terms if he knows the meaning and the dialectic of the process and clearly appreciates what he is seeking to do. Handbooks and guides to cases can never substitute for this sound appreciation, and thinking Protestants will resist like the plague a clamor for them.

If this book helps those who read it to appreciate Protestant casuistry as a process for relating faith to life, it will have done its work. The success it may enjoy in this undertaking should bring credit to those from whom the author has gained whatever spiritual insights he has about the problem. His debt to those who have guided his quest is apparent in the text. The reader may be sure that it is felt more deeply on the personal level than is expressed in the printed page.

Likewise, more specific debt to those who have helped in the actual preparation of this work should be acknowledged. I refrain from naming them lest they be blamed for things not their fault. Their criticism, counsel, and encouragement have sustained the author in this present undertaking. I rejoice to know them as friends in Christ and as fellow workers in the task of making real to our age the implication of the eternal gospel of Jesus Christ.

Blacksburg, Virginia
Spring, 1953

                                                    E.L.L., JR.

PART
I

THE CONCEPT OF CASUISTRY

CHAPTER I

The Meaning of Casuistry

IT IS not easy to be a Christian in an unchristian world. The Christian faith places those who are obedient to Christ under an ethical demand frequently in conflict with the standards of the world about them. Moreover, Christians who are wholeheartedly devoted to Christ find themselves perplexed as they seek to determine what their faith requires in the everyday decisions of life.

Many people are conscious of a gap between their faith as Christians and their daily actions, between the professions of their worship and the actions of their lives. Others give an unconscious witness to this gap in their offhand conversations. The pew frequently complains of idealistic pulpit utterances which give little guidance for life in the " harsh " worlds of politics and commerce. The pulpit, perhaps in retaliation, blames the pew for not manifesting distinctive Christian behavior in the secular affairs of men. Once a congregation has scattered after the Sunday service it returns to the workaday world much as a drop of dye returns to an ocean, losing all distinctiveness.

Admonitions to be loyal to Christ come cheaply when couched in vague and general terms. But they are difficult, and often resisted sharply, when spelled out in pertinent detail. Devotion to Christ is difficult in a non-Christian and even anti-Christian world. It is difficult not only because moral stamina and effort are required to maintain such devotion, but also because agonized and prayerful consideration is required in order to decide what the obedient conscience requires in practical and daily situations. Should a Christian participate in modern mass weapon warfare? How should he vote in an election? What should be his attitude toward the new housing development in his town, toward the Negroes moving in down the street, toward the selling of obscene literature at the corner newsstand? These questions, representative of hundreds like them, must be faced if Christians are to make a relevant impact upon social conditions around them.

Christians are constrained by their faith to be obedient to Christ. This obedience bridges the gulf between faith and works by compelling faith to issue in works. Christians must show forth the love of Christ, a love which they know both as the nature of God and as the key to genuine community and fellowship among men. But how shall men live according to Christian love in a world that dishonors the Christian way even in places where it honors the Christian name? The process of answering this question is known as casuistry. Casuistry is the branch of theology that seeks to relate what is demanded by the ultimate standards of the Christian ethic to what can be expected of men in the particular situations of common life. Philosophers, speaking in abstract terms, define casuistry as the application of ethical principles to specific cases. Agonizing consciences, trying to lead a Christian life in a sinful and difficult world, are apt to call it the process of making compromises. Whatever be the definition, the reality is inescapable. All Christians are engaged, if only by default, in the process of relating their faith to the world in which they live.

We are speaking of casuistry in the broad sense. It is the process by which every moral system relates itself to concrete decisions. John T. McNeill describes the process as follows:

" Elemental casuistry is a matter of everyday moral living. (We are speaking here of casuistry in the moral, not in the legal, sense.)

It is morality in detail. It arises where reasoned answers are presented on the courses of action morally advisable in given cases. The activated conscience asks for reasoned solutions of its moral dilemmas, made in accord with broad underlying beliefs which lie beyond the area of dilemma. Casuistry does not determine or create these basic beliefs: its function is to apply them to emergent cases. Every parent is a casuist to his inquiring child when he explains why some act is good or bad " (" Casuistry in the Puritan Age," in *Religion in Life,* Winter, 1942–1943, p. 77).

Of course the name of the process is not all-important. The word " casuistry " has many sinister connotations from which it needs to be rescued before it can be of use in the contemporary Church. But the word is traditional in the history of the Church and basic to theological discourse. We shall use it boldly, not only as a useful term for a process that is genuinely a part of Christian ethics, but as a word rightfully a part of our theological heritage. We are interested in that dialectic of Christian experience by which a person comes to terms with the Christian imperative on the one hand and the situation in which he lives on the other.

All ethical living involves a tension between what men ought to do and what they can do. All morality is founded upon the interchange between ideal norms and actual behavior. Men are goaded to ethical works by the urge to bring their conduct into conformity with their ideals. Without a striving for good conduct morality dies.

Even in cases where men set their own standards of right and wrong there is a tension between the professed ideals and the actual behavior of the group. Man has a strange capacity to seek things that are beyond him, to set goals and objectives after which he constantly may strive. He has an even stranger capacity to feel remorse when he does not attain these goals, to harbor a sense of failure and guilt whenever he has defaulted in his loyalty to them.

What is true about ethics in general is the more true about religious ethics, and especially true about Christian ethics. Biblical faith presents men with a demand from above, a demand which is far beyond their possible achievement. The demand comes, not from human standards, but from divine dictation. It is not a norm of expediency, compelling only when men deem allegiance to it wise or profitable. Christianity boldly proclaims the high level of its demand, a demand that draws men beyond themselves. Every concrete moral act must be brought under its scrutiny. Men must strive to adhere to this high standard or be judged apostate.

Insistence upon the continuing and absolute quality of God's expectations of man is one of the essential elements in the Biblical message. Prophets and preachers, even more than systematic theologians, enunciate the imperatives of God's holy will with insistent zeal. God requires justice, mercy, and truth, not because they are pleasant ideals which keep life happy and decent, but because they are the marks of obedience to a righteous Creator. As Amos puts it:

"Even though you offer me your burnt offerings and cereal offerings,
    I will not accept them,
and the peace offerings of your fatted beasts I will not look upon.
Take away from me the noise of your songs;
    to the melody of your harps I will not listen.
But let justice roll down like waters,
    and righteousness like an ever-flowing stream"
(Ch. 5:22–24, R. S. V.).

The norm of Christian ethics is the kind of love seen in the life and death of Christ. As seen supremely in his cross, this norm is so high as to breed a provisional despair of fulfillment by mortal men. Christian love is not the imaginative projection of good-intentioned human fancy; it is the supreme way of the incarnate God. In the cross we have a revelation of

God's self-giving love for men, and in the Gospels a clear injunction that we too take up our crosses in the service of Christ. Such revelation far outstrips the usual extent of human capacity. Most men do not lay down their lives for their friends, let alone for those who revile and persecute them. The cross of Christ sharply contradicts the normal expectations of worldly wisdom, but it remains the very beginning and end of Christian ethics.

" In this the love of God was made manifest among us, that God sent his only Son into the world, so that we might live through him. In this is love, not that we loved God but that he loved us and sent his Son to be the expiation for our sins. Beloved, if God so loved us, we also ought to love one another " (I John 4:9-11, R. S. V.).

Some years ago the Swedish theologian Anders Nygren put the theological world in his debt with a study of the distinctive quality of Christian love. According to Nygren, *agape* (which is the special word for love in the New Testament) is distinct from *eros* (which is the general Greek word for love). *Agape* is the love of God made known in Christ; it is unsolicited and unmerited by the objects of that love; it is forgetful of its own interest and seeks no rewards for its own sake. *Eros,* on the other hand, is self-regarding love; it is the love of men who seek benefits from love; it is merited by those who are its object; it expects a reward — not a crass reward to be sure, but a reward befitting the nature of love. The distinction between these two types of love is best understood as the gulf between a love that man might achieve in his highest moments and a love that God alone has the power to make known to the world.

Father M. C. D'Arcy, a Jesuit, has more recently modified Nygren's thesis by suggesting that both types of love may have human expression, and that in human conduct they are often mixed together. For instance, the relationship between man and wife involves elements of both *eros* and *agape*. But D'Arcy's line of argument still admits of a distinction between the divine standard and human conduct. All human marriages are less than they might be by the standard of God, and marriage counselors and judges must often deal with problems apparently lacking even the slightest resemblance to the ideal of love.

It is this apparently abstract, yet crucial, distinction between a divinely given and a humanly determined norm that creates a special need for casuistry in the Christian ethic. The demands of Christian love must be translated into strategies applicable to a world corrupted by human sin. The " way of love " does not, save by careful translation of its implications into other categories, adjudicate the types of claims that arise between parties in industrial disputes or settle conflicts between nations that are fighting one another on the basis of self-interest. In the blunt and forceful words of Alfred North Whitehead: " As society is now constituted a literal allegiance to the moral precepts scattered throughout the Gospels would mean sudden death " (*Adventures of Ideas,* p. 18. The Macmillan Company, 1933).

" As society is now constituted " — with this phrase Whitehead touches the basic problem. Christian obedience is not a simple possibility in a disobedient world. The conscience is forced to compromise in order to act by choosing actions that are less than perfect expressions of the standard to which it gives full devotion. Christian faith understands the tension between the way of Christ and the way of the world, not only because the demand of God is high, but because the performance of man is low. Man is estranged from God; he turns his back upon the demands of love. There is a law in his members, to use the phrase of Saint Paul, that wars against the law in his mind. Even the will to love has been impaired by sin.

Christianity is a redemptive religion claiming to save men from the power of sin over their lives. Faith reorients the disobedience of men into obedience to Christ and creates new beings loyal to the claims of Christian love and dedicated to its ends. But, far from removing the perplexities, this new devotion increases them. How is a new convert to express his obedience to Christ as he seeks to act as a loyal disciple in a disobedient and unchristian world? Christians must relate the love which they know in Christ to the strife and bickering which mark so much of the world. Those who take seriously the constraint of love face many problems as they seek to relate that love to a world that disrespects and dishonors it.

If the standard by which Christians are to live were set up by men on the basis of human wisdom, it could be altered to meet the exigencies of given cases. It could be changed to " make sense " or to " work " in practical situations. But the standard of Christian faith is divinely given; it cannot be tailored or watered down. It always stands in judgment over men's actions. When men transgress a humanly created norm, it is possible to say that it doesn't matter, but when they transgress the will of God, they are always judged as having sinned against his majesty.

Though ultimate in its demand, the Christian imperative is nevertheless relevant. Its claims cannot be dismissed because they seem impossible of complete attainment. Love requires of men that they do whatever they can do in the situation in which they find themselves to express their faithful obedience to Christ. Even in its divine givenness Christian love is related to human history. In the work and death of Christ the norms of Christian faith were expressed in human actions. The ideals were made real through an incarnation. Christian devotion must consequently bear the actual burdens of its next-door neighbors even while it witnesses to an unstinting and unceasing demand above all human actions. It must give the cup of cold water to the stranger in the name of Christ's love for all mankind. This earth-bound, decision-bound, practical side of the Christian ethic is no less a factor demanding casuistry than is the high nature of the Christian norm that makes it appear so unattainable in a sinful world. Casuistry is the process of deciding how to relate the demand of love to the actual service of the neighbor. Abstract philosophies may be permitted the luxury of contemplating beautiful ideals, but Christian love must find a practical ministry for living men. This requires us to take up burdens in the service of Christ and express love in relationship to the hard and realistic world about us.

This urge to concrete, immediately tangible, and historically pertinent action can never be separated from the ultimate demands of Christian love. Each must be related to the other. Christian love expresses its high and final devotion in concrete and practical activity; in fact, it is only through such activity that its devotion can be expressed.

" There is no lack of recognition in the churches that love is the norm of Christian living. But love is interpreted and understood in such a way that it does not call for strenuous engagement in the perennial knock-down drag-out maneuverings for a decent ordering of social and economic and political relationships. How do we harness the love which most church members acknowledge to be the gospel's demand on them to the public responsibilities which so many of them side-step? " (Cornelius Loew, " Rethinking Fundamentals," in *Christianity and Society,* Autumn, 1951, p. 9).

The answer to the question ending this quotation is fraught with difficulty. The difficulty appears, not only in arousing men to their responsibility, but in knowing exactly what that responsibility is at any given time. The choices that men face are seldom black and white, but various shades of gray. The task of conscience is more than to guide them to the clear path of right; it is to help men to choose the best of several alternatives which are before them. The conscience must learn to handle the problem of compromise, the sacrificing of one value in order to serve another.

Some men argue that no guidance is possible, in terms of previously agreed upon principles, for dealing with these problems. Others are very certain what constitutes Christian conduct for every type of situation. Both groups, however, note the contrast between " God's design " and " man's disorder " and acknowledge the necessity of translating into practical terms the demands of Christian love. Both evolve for themselves a strategy for dealing with this problem — that is, a casuistry.

Those who want a code book for Christian living will not find one in this present work. Those who believe that Christian freedom must be bound by no principles of action will be a bit impatient with the whole effort of this book. These two positions ought to correct each other. Those who seek too precise a set of rules embrace a more Catholic approach and tend to codify the norms of Christian behavior into a legalism. Those who deny the rules frequently represent an aberration of Protestantism which forgets that men need standards for their conduct and principles for their behavior. Nels Ferré, in commenting upon these matters, observes:

" Some modern theologians affirm that Christianity has no such principles [for relating true, i.e., ideal, society to actual society] at all, but must, rather, obediently answer its Lord in concrete situations, directly and with ever new freshness of insight and daring. Others, on the opposite side, reduce Christian ethics to a matter of mere rational choices, founded upon the most inclusive good. Both sides are guilty of man's basic fallacy, a false either-or. For there are such revelational norms as are implicit in the holy gospel of God's *agape* and the involvement of the full fellowship love " (*Christianity and Society*, p. 59. Harper & Brothers, 1950).

Protestant casuistry in particular will tend to shy from detailed prescriptions, preferring to err on the side of flexibility and uncertainty rather than that of legalism and absurdity. Protestantism will never produce precise codes by which sin and virtue can be uncontestedly separated and degrees of penance be balanced against the relative seriousness of particular sins. But it can produce a basic set of understandings that make the ethics of evangelical faith more than a hit-and-miss affair. It can develop a basic pattern for relating the norms of faith to concrete ethical decisions. Such a pattern is casuistry in the best sense of the term. No escape is possible from this process. Casuistry is like faith itself: even if one denies that he has it, he has the conviction of his denial. It is like a liturgy: if one rejects a formal type, he will find a substitute, perhaps no less rigid. Because of the ultimate character of its ethical norm, and also because of its genuine concern for the actual conditions of the world, Christian ethics will always be involved in casuistry in the broad moral sense. In reality (if not in name), casuistry is an inescapable part of the Christian life. Only through acknowledgment of this fact can we be sure of seeking to apply the norms of faith to problems that confront us in the world.

CHAPTER II

Our Distrust of Casuistry

THE mere mention of casuistry in many Protestant circles uncovers a deep-seated distrust of the term. Casuistry is regarded as the legalism of evasion by which priests in a confessional can salve the consciences of parishioners without requiring a radical change in their lives. It is castigated as the device used by the Jesuits to dodge their Christian duty. It is taken as the mark of Pharisees in every age — the way of those who tithe mint, anise, and cummin but neglect weightier matters of the law.

" Moreover," runs the argument against casuistry, " is not the difficulty of the contemporary Church its ethical lukewarmness? Surely a process defined from one perspective as the science of necessary compromise will not correct this malady! There is already too much compromise of Christian standards; the problem is not to learn how more effectively to deal with the problem of compromise, but rather to learn how to avoid it. Christians need a renewed devotion to Christ's way, not sophisticated rationalizations as to why his way cannot be directly applied to the world in which we live."

This argument expresses a contempt for casuistry prevalent in the Church. Not only is casuistry regarded as being unessential to Christian ethics, but alien and dangerous as well. Reaction to the term is usually unfavorable and often antagonistic. Seldom considered essential to Christian living, casuistry is thought to destroy all that is ethically vital in the Christian faith. Indeed, Webster's second definition of the term articulates what men commonly take to be the only meaning: " sophistical, equivocal, or specious reasoning, . . . especially in regard to law or morals."

Some of this distrust is rightly founded, but the rest is based upon misconceptions that should be acknowledged and overcome. Distrust of casuistry as a scheme of moral evasion is, to a large measure, a justifiable reaction against the machinations of the medieval Jesuits. Casuistry in the Jesuit sense was a means to the advancement of nominal Christian conversion on a mass scale. In order to win converts from a morally lax Europe without requiring of them too great an ethical regeneration, Jesuit casuistry was devised as a way to accommodate the moral ideals of Christian faith to the conditions of the time. In this situation sinister connotations were given to the term, and it came to stand for opportunism in, and perversion of, the Christian ethic.

Jesuit ethics involved the doctrine of probabilism, the use of which did much to corrupt the life of the medieval Church. According to the doctrine of probabilism, when the moral status of a particular action is questionable (i.e., not absolutely forbidden), the conscience may approve the action, even though the more probable and usual opinion may favor an opposite and contradictory action. When laxly or cynically applied, this doctrine has the effect of making all actions lawful except those which are specifically condemned by Church authority because they contradict the " natural law." Pascal's *Lettres Provinciales* are the *locus classicus* of protest against the laxity and abuses which sprang up on the basis of probabilism as promulgated in the seventeenth century. Pascal's criticism of the Jesuits and those who followed them is sharp and biting:

" Let them seriously ponder, as in the sight of God, how shameful, and how prejudicial to the Church, is the morality which you casuists are in the habit of propagating; the scandalous and unmeasured license which they are introducing into public manners; the obstinate and violent hardihood with which you support them. And if they do not think it full time to rise against such disorders, their blindness is as much to be pitied as yours, fathers; and you and they have equal reason to dread that saying of Saint Augustine, founded on the words of Jesus Christ, in the Gospel: Woe to the blind leaders! woe to the blind followers! " (Letter XI).

Saint Alphonsus Liguori, though having originally defended the doctrine of probabilism, modified it for the sake of sanity by requiring that the two actions in question be of equal probability — that is, that the case be as strong for the one chosen as for the one rejected. He avoided both the looseness of probabilism (which could choose any probable course of action regardless of the relative weight in favor of one particular course) and the strictness of probabiliorism (which could take no action unless one side was definitely more probable than another). In this contribution of Liguori, known as equiprobabilism, both excessive rigor and excessive laxity were supposedly avoided. By requiring that the chosen course of action be at least as probable as the rejected course of action, Liguori made some place for the norm or standard without losing sight of the ambiguities and difficulties involved in deciding how particular norms are to be expressed in concrete human situations.

Though the Christian conscience rightly protests the Jesuit corruptions, the system of casuistry in Jesuit moral theology is not without understandable reasons for development. In the midst of social and political life directed by the Church some means is necessary for relating the final norm of the Christian ethic to the concrete problems of social life. Many of these problems do not pose clear-cut cases of conformity to, or violation of, specific Christian standards, but are questionable cases in which one must weigh imponderables and make tentative decisions apart from any clear understanding of the course of action for which Christian love calls. The casuistry of probabilism, for all its misuse as a means to justify accommodation, furnished a way

to deal with cases of conscience in which there was outright uncertainty as to the nature of a Christian choice. It was a scheme
by which, for instance, the moral theologian could regard as
ethically justified a decision to vote on either side of an average
American political contest. The system of Jesuit casuistry attempted to devise some sort of way to deal with the compromises which are necessary in relating the problems of daily
existence to the demands of Christian norms. Alas, it too frequently " watered down " the demands of the Christian ethic in
order to adapt it to the low moral condition of medieval Europe.

Modern men are perhaps the less patient with the Jesuits because they fail to recognize the problems their order faced. In
the medieval period all of life was under the conscious rule of
the Church. The Jesuits were mixed up with the world as rep-
resentatives of religion; they could not practice a religious ethic
on Sunday and another ethic the rest of the week. Ethical
choices in modern life, especially the daily ones, are often made
without reference to religious standards. In modern secular culture a sharp division is found between the complex situations
in which daily moral choices are made and the realm of religious faith. The average man in the street, even the average
churchgoer, has lost the sense of tension between Christian
norms and the cultural conditions that surround him. Common
life is no longer brought under complete and rigorous Christian scrutiny. The compromises of Christian love which men
make by such commonly accepted practices as waging war and
manipulating economic processes for their own self-interest
are not recognized as compromises. These belong to the hard,
real world into which religion " should not meddle." Modern
man too often relegates the compromises involved in the harsh
side of life to the level of secular strategy, whereas the Jesuit
was necessarily involved in these compromises as an expression
of religious faith.

The secularization of contemporary culture in no sense removes the compromises the Jesuits faced. It simply bypasses them as far as religion is concerned by leaving society and its problems to another realm. This is a dodge rather than a solution to the problem. It places life and faith in two distinct compartments and allows no Christian concern to express itself on the social problems of our day.

No group in recent times has felt the contrast between secular standards and the gospel norm more acutely than the adherents of what is usually called the social gospel. They genuinely aimed to break down this contradiction and proposed to Christianize the social order. When Walter Rauschenbusch, the leading spirit of the social gospel movement, developed his theology, he said:

"The social gospel is the old message of salvation, but enlarged and intensified. The individualistic gospel has taught us to see the sinfulness of every human heart and has inspired us with faith in the willingness and power of God to save every soul that comes to him. But it has not given us an adequate understanding of the sinfulness of the social order and its share in the sins of all individuals within it. It has not evoked faith in the will and power of God to redeem the permanent institutions of human society from their inherited guilt of oppression and extortion" (*A Theology for the Social Gospel*, p. 5. The Macmillan Company, 1947).

There is a driving Christian urge behind this effort to bring all the spheres of human life under the control of Christian standards. The social gospel movement was motivated by a genuine Christian concern to overcome the wide gulf between Christian faith, with its high conception of human brotherhood, and the life of Christians, whose conduct in the secularized worlds of business and politics bore little apparent resemblance to their professions of religious faith.

The social gospel thrived in a period of general and widespread optimism. It shared the hopefulness of an age that had emerged from a world war which had been won by those dedicated to making the world "safe for democracy." It was shocked by human suffering in a way in which our age, accustomed and callous to oppression, want, and cruelty, is no longer shocked.

This optimism was not measured by the lack of a conception of sin in the theology of the movement. The leaders of the social gospel knew the power of sin and bravely castigated those who were making private gain at social expense. The optimism of the social gospel was apparent, rather, in its trust that Christian love could be translated into social reality without a process of compromise. From the perspective of an idealistic Christianity it oversimplified the problem of relating faith to culture. The leaders of this movement did not reckon with the necessity of a casuistry but regarded the application of Christian love to the social order as a straightforward affair. They took the ultimate norm of Christian love as equivalent to a practical program of action. They thereby contributed to the distrust of casuistry, not by perverting it, but by denying the necessity for it.

The distrust of casuistry was evident in this movement, not only in the assumption that Christian love was directly applicable to social situations, but also in an explicit scorn of the casuistry of the Pharisees. The teachings of Jesus were regarded as a wholesale rejection of the whole casuistic process. Rauschenbusch put it this way:

" [The social gospel] scorns the tithing of mint, anise, and cummin, at which the Pharisees are still busy, and insists on getting down to the weightier matters of God's law, to justice and mercy. It ties up religion not only with duty, but with big duty that stirs the soul with religious feeling and throws it back on God for help. . . . The Kingdom of God can be established by nothing except righteous life and action (*ibid.*, p. 15)."

The sensitive Christian conscience cannot but share the motive of this passage. Surely a legalism which places petty and

inconsequential matters in place of the great concerns which ought to mark religion has little place in Christian faith. But our question must be whether the error of the Pharisees actually lay in the fact that they used a casuistry, or whether their error lay in the purposes they sought to serve with its use.

The casuistry of the Pharisees differed in purpose from that of the Jesuits. In the case of the Jesuits casuistry was a means of moral evasion, designed to make Church membership possible on the basis of a minimal standard of personal virtue. In the case of the Pharisees casuistry was a necessary extension of the basically moralistic religion of the law, made necessary by the constant need to modify a rigid code in face of particular situations. Thus, while the Jesuit casuistry took the form of probabilism, allowing every action not specifically condemned, the casuistry of the Pharisees took the form of legalism, condemning (at least by implication) every action not specifically allowed.

It is not hard to find illustrations of the absurdities to which this legalism led — " how some knots and not others could be tied on the Sabbath, [how] vinegar, if swallowed, could be used to relieve a sore throat but it could not be gargled " (Harry Emerson Fosdick, *The Man from Nazareth,* p. 76. Harper & Brothers, 1949). But, it is possible to pass a fair judgment upon the Pharisees only if one understands the basic purpose of their legalistic system. The code morality of the Jews was used to protect the religious community from pollution by the moral degeneracy surrounding it. The rules tended to be strict rather than lax, and transgressions were religious rather than simply ethical offenses. As external pressures on the Jewish community grew more intense and allegiance to the ceremonial and moral code was increasingly made the mark of orthodoxy, the law became an intolerable burden if one sought to obey it in every detail. The Pharisees, the liberal rather than the conservative party of the time, were prompted by humanitarian ends to pro-

The Rediscovery of Casuistry

Since the period of the social gospel the climate of theological opinion has been greatly modified. Even as the social gospel was a reaction against individualistic and otherworldly conservatism, so much of the present mood is a reaction against the social gospel. Where reaction against the social gospel has reached an extreme form, Christian social passion has tended to wither. Where the social gospel has been qualified without being totally rejected, there has appeared a concern to relate Christian faith to social problems which has been accompanied by a sober recognition of the contrast between the Christian ideal and what can actually be done in given situations.

Many of the leaders of this new orientation, which for want of a more precise name may be called "neo-orthodoxy," are heirs of the social gospel. They share its urge to make Christian love relevant to social issues, but they part company with the assumption that a straight uncompromised application of love to social problems is generally possible. This new mood, cultivated as a result of two world wars and their aftermath, is aware of the ambiguities and necessary compromise involved in Christian social action. It freely acknowledges our apparent inability to bring the institutions of human society under the clear and simple direction of Christian love. Idealistic preaching which merely proclaims that the way of love ought to rule in the world is now criticized as irrelevant to the harsh realities of social action. Out of this new perspective has sprung a not-

inconsequential matters in place of the great concerns which ought to mark religion has little place in Christian faith. But our question must be whether the error of the Pharisees actually lay in the fact that they used a casuistry, or whether their error lay in the purposes they sought to serve with its use.

The casuistry of the Pharisees differed in purpose from that of the Jesuits. In the case of the Jesuits casuistry was a means of moral evasion, designed to make Church membership possible on the basis of a minimal standard of personal virtue. In the case of the Pharisees casuistry was a necessary extension of the basically moralistic religion of the law, made necessary by the constant need to modify a rigid code in face of particular situations. Thus, while the Jesuit casuistry took the form of probabilism, allowing every action not specifically condemned, the casuistry of the Pharisees took the form of legalism, condemning (at least by implication) every action not specifically allowed.

It is not hard to find illustrations of the absurdities to which this legalism led — " how some knots and not others could be tied on the Sabbath, [how] vinegar, if swallowed, could be used to relieve a sore throat but it could not be gargled " (Harry Emerson Fosdick, *The Man from Nazareth,* p. 76. Harper & Brothers, 1949). But, it is possible to pass a fair judgment upon the Pharisees only if one understands the basic purpose of their legalistic system. The code morality of the Jews was used to protect the religious community from pollution by the moral degeneracy surrounding it. The rules tended to be strict rather than lax, and transgressions were religious rather than simply ethical offenses. As external pressures on the Jewish community grew more intense and allegiance to the ceremonial and moral code was increasingly made the mark of orthodoxy, the law became an intolerable burden if one sought to obey it in every detail. The Pharisees, the liberal rather than the conservative party of the time, were prompted by humanitarian ends to pro-

The Rediscovery of Casuistry

SINCE the period of the social gospel the climate of theological opir.ion has been greatly modified. Even as the social gospel was a reaction against individualistic and otherworldly conservatism, so much of the present mood is a reaction against the social gospel. Where reaction against the social gospel has reached an extreme form, Christian social passion has tended to wither. Where the social gospel has been qualified without being totally rejected, there has appeared a concern to relate Christian faith to social problems which has been accompanied by a sober recognition of the contrast between the Christian ideal and what can actually be done in given situations.

Many of the leaders of this new orientation, which for want of a more precise name may be called "neo-orthodoxy," are heirs of the social gospel. They share its urge to make Christian love relevant to social issues, but they part company with the assumption that a straight uncompromised application of love to social problems is generally possible. This new mood, cultivated as a result of two world wars and their aftermath, is aware of the ambiguities and necessary compromise involved in Christian social action. It freely acknowledges our apparent inability to bring the institutions of human society under the clear and simple direction of Christian love. Idealistic preaching which merely proclaims that the way of love ought to rule in the world is now criticized as irrelevant to the harsh realities of social action. Out of this new perspective has sprung a not-

inconsequential matters in place of the great concerns which ought to mark religion has little place in Christian faith. But our question must be whether the error of the Pharisees actually lay in the fact that they used a casuistry, or whether their error lay in the purposes they sought to serve with its use.

The casuistry of the Pharisees differed in purpose from that of the Jesuits. In the case of the Jesuits casuistry was a means of moral evasion, designed to make Church membership possible on the basis of a minimal standard of personal virtue. In the case of the Pharisees casuistry was a necessary extension of the basically moralistic religion of the law, made necessary by the constant need to modify a rigid code in face of particular situations. Thus, while the Jesuit casuistry took the form of probabilism, allowing every action not specifically condemned, the casuistry of the Pharisees took the form of legalism, condemning (at least by implication) every action not specifically allowed.

It is not hard to find illustrations of the absurdities to which this legalism led — " how some knots and not others could be tied on the Sabbath, [how] vinegar, if swallowed, could be used to relieve a sore throat but it could not be gargled " (Harry Emerson Fosdick, *The Man from Nazareth,* p. 76. Harper & Brothers, 1949). But, it is possible to pass a fair judgment upon the Pharisees only if one understands the basic purpose of their legalistic system. The code morality of the Jews was used to protect the religious community from pollution by the moral degeneracy surrounding it. The rules tended to be strict rather than lax, and transgressions were religious rather than simply ethical offenses. As external pressures on the Jewish community grew more intense and allegiance to the ceremonial and moral code was increasingly made the mark of orthodoxy, the law became an intolerable burden if one sought to obey it in every detail. The Pharisees, the liberal rather than the conservative party of the time, were prompted by humanitarian ends to pro-

vide a casuistry in accord with which specific needs of men could be met within the limits of the rigid code. Since they desired to remain within the framework of the law, the only possible expression of this humane spirit was through a casuistry. The casuistry provided a freedom under the law to meet the demands of special circumstances. Foolish as was the content of Pharisaical casuistry, it is possible to see it as the only thing that tempered the rigidity of the law.

The social gospel, moreover, was impatient with legalism, not only in its ancient Pharisaical expression, but in contemporary " puritanical " expressions. Much of the Church, particularly in America, had carried over from the Puritans, not their broadly conceived attempt to bring all community life under religious oversight, but a series of restrictions unimaginatively applied and long since devoid of their original meaning. Cardplaying, originally prohibited as an effort to prevent the spread of gambling, came to be scorned simply on the basis of tradition. Similarly, arbitrary prohibitions of smoking, dancing, and drinking were made the marks of Christian conduct. Hence had arisen a new legalism, which like the legalism of the Pharisees, concentrated attention on external marks of virtue and neglected weightier matters of faith and practice.

The liberal spirit of the social gospel movement was critical of the private type of salvation offered by traditional conservatism. It rightly understood that a gospel of individual salvation, coupled to an ethic of rigid but petty morality, is hardly a carrier of the best in Christian living. Liberalism would have none of such a chopped down private goodness. It understood the relevance of Christian faith to all of life and helped to make a great deal of modern Christianity publicly concerned and socially outgoing. Rauschenbusch and his followers prepared the way for the social emphasis in the best of subsequent theology. Their protest against individual otherworldliness in the ethics of Christian conservatism was true to the very heart of our faith.

Casuistry in both its Jesuit and Pharisaical forms was part of a legalistic type of religion. But casuistry is a more inclusive reality and includes the process of expressing ideal norms through concrete actions in any system. Let us not ignore the examples of the Jesuits and Pharisees, for from them we can learn the corruptions to which casuistry is prone. But let us not be so foolish as to reject all attempts to find a valid casuistry for applying Christian norms to common life, as though to burn the orchard because the trees are attacked by insects at certain seasons of the year. Our distrust of casuistry can help greatly if it does not turn into an absolute rejection of it. It can help us to avoid both moral evasion and harsh legalism and to steer a sensible course in seeking to apply the Christian ethic to common life.

LIBRARY ROOM
CINCINNATI BAPTIST BIBLE COLLEGE
CINCINNATI, OHIO

CHAPTER **III**

The Rediscovery of Casuistry

SINCE the period of the social gospel the climate of theological opirion has been greatly modified. Even as the social gospel was a reaction against individualistic and otherworldly conservatism, so much of the present mood is a reaction against the social gospel. Where reaction against the social gospel has reached an extreme form, Christian social passion has tended to wither. Where the social gospel has been qualified without being totally rejected, there has appeared a concern to relate Christian faith to social problems which has been accompanied by a sober recognition of the contrast between the Christian ideal and what can actually be done in given situations.

Many of the leaders of this new orientation, which for want of a more precise name may be called " neo-orthodoxy," are heirs of the social gospel. They share its urge to make Christian love relevant to social issues, but they part company with the assumption that a straight uncompromised application of love to social problems is generally possible. This new mood, cultivated as a result of two world wars and their aftermath, is aware of the ambiguities and necessary compromise involved in Christian social action. It freely acknowledges our apparent inability to bring the institutions of human society under the clear and simple direction of Christian love. Idealistic preaching which merely proclaims that the way of love ought to rule in the world is now criticized as irrelevant to the harsh realities of social action. Out of this new perspective has sprung a not-always-bridled polemic against too easy a belief in the " work-ability of love " and too simple a set of formulas for applying love to the concrete needs of society.

Under the impact of the neo-orthodox outlook, thinking in Christian ethics is now aware of the reality of compromise and thoroughly conversant with the tension between the ideal and the actual. Because of the polemical context in which they have been argued, these insights have been so overemphasized at times that neo-orthodoxy has been called a theology of despair. This counterpolemic does little except to becloud the issue and obscure the importance of neo-orthodoxy's contribution to social ethics. It has made Christian thinkers aware of the basic under-standing that underlies a system of casuistry. Now theologians are sensitive to the reality of compromise that marks casuistry, even though they rarely use the term or spell out the implica-tions of the concept in defined detail. The cutting edge of con-temporary theology no longer is marked by a distrust of casuist-ry such as existed during the two decades between world wars. It may even be hoped that casuistry will be rediscovered as a legitimate term in the vocabulary of Christian ethics.

The main contribution of the neo-orthodox movement sharp-ens the sense of the contrast between the norm of love and the actions of men. It understands the compromises involved in every human decision and the inadequacy of any social institu-tion to embody the total demands of Christian love. Any re-discovery of casuistry in the Church will be indebted to an ap-preciation of this tension. Unless the standard of Christian ethics is recognized as an ultimate standard of God, then one pole in the casuistic reference is lacking; unless the compromise neces-sarily present in every historical decision is understood, the other pole is missing. Neo-orthodox theology brings special sensitivity regarding both the ultimate demands of Christian love and the partial and sinful decisions of men. In its doctrine of God it provides a sense of his majesty and the limitless requirements of his holy will; in its doctrine of sin it makes men aware of the compromises that exist in all human attempts to serve that will.

Casuistry must be more than the understanding of the compromise involved in relating love to the sinful conditions of society. Casuistry, in order to be genuine, must be concerned with principles and relationships between the ultimate and proximate levels of ethical decision. There is a tendency in some forms of neo-orthodoxy to do away with all such principles, to emphasize the place of immediate decisions and to minimize the role of systematic understanding. The tendency springs from the philosophical assumptions of the movement, assumptions founded in the temper of existentialism. Just as existentialism seeks to know truths of immediate personal meaning, but not general truths of overarching validity, so in its ethical life it attempts to make decisions without formulating principles or having rules. This procedure evidences a desire to do what circumstances dictate, but it tends to let the circumstances rather than the principle guide its conduct. This can result in a type of ethical relativism which, while not cynical in the usual sense, is nevertheless unable to draw well-defined lines between right and wrong.

The idea of having a casuistry will not be welcomed by thinkers who disavow all principles for guiding conduct. For them there can be no demarcation of the type of actions that love requires save the guidance perceived in the immediate situation of faith. God may require of the conscience one type of behavior today and another type tomorrow, or even two types of behavior in seeming contradiction with each other.

The guidance that comes from an ethic that scorns all rules is insufficient. It responds to God in such a varying set of decisions as to leave the Christian without any distinctive set of standards. Such a relativism is hardly to be preferred to its opposite, a legalism that is too narrow in its definition of " Christian" conduct. On the other hand, even the "principle" of having no principles may nurture a set of characteristic reactions all its own. Adherents of the doctrine of immediate decision may actually display a special and distinctive attitude toward many questions, doing so without even acknowledging that they have such an attitude. When this happens, the individuals concerned are involved in self-contradiction.

But even as one affirms the place of principles, he must be careful to know their possible limitations. There are situations in which violations of general principles are demanded by more ultimate considerations. The most illuminating experiences with this type of situation were those of the illegal resistance movements that worked under totalitarian regimes. Under the Nazi regime during World War II, as under Communist regimes today, courageous Christians have found it necessary to engage in acts of resistance to the State that under normal circumstances would contradict all they have been taught to honor. The story of Dietrich Bonhoeffer is a case in point. Bonhoeffer was a young German Christian who lived during the rise of Hitlerism. As he came to see that Christians bear social responsibility, he was attracted by Gandhi's movement, and for a time he considered going to India to study it. Prompted by a generally pacifist outlook, he saw in Hitler's military despotism the negation of all Christian values and came steadfastly to oppose the rising power. Despite his general convictions about the taking of life, however, he was finally led to believe that Germany could be saved only by the assassination of Hitler. Executed by the Nazis for his participation in a plot on Hitler's life, he became a martyr for an act that contradicted his own normal standards.

Action like that to which Bonhoeffer finally came is a last consideration, not an initial one; the normal situation of the Christian is to proceed in accord with a set of accepted standards. There is no justification for using the abnormal situation to argue for the rejection of all standards. Surely a place must be left in Christian living for desperate and heroic exceptions to the rules. But where this kind of action becomes the only action sought after, men are left without the creative and stabilizing influence of commonly accepted standards. They are left with no grounds to vindicate their actions save appeal to the success of their own struggle to pursue them. This leads to an evaporation of standards and commonly ends in a morality of pure force.

A breakdown of standards such as has appeared in the totalitarian countries has also infected the democratic West, explaining in part the degeneration of its morality, both personal and social. Symptoms of this malady appear as political corruption in high places, as political campaigns designed to sway crowds with smears and slogans rather than to argue issues, and as the frame of mind in which capital and labor find themselves forced to contend with each other as antagonists because of an inability to negotiate on commonly accepted grounds of justice and truth. For normal and creative democratic living we need standards of fairness and honesty. For normal Christian behavior we must be guided by a casuistry in which a set of principles is acknowledged as a guiding framework, but a framework always subject to, and never a substitute for, the ultimate demand of love.

To argue that we need principles in casuistry leads naturally to a new set of considerations. Overemphasis upon the role of principles is a mark of legalism; underemphasis is the mark of antinomianism, which is its opposite. Various traditions in the history of the Church have fallen into one or the other of these errors. Roman Catholicism, together with a type of perfectionism such as has sometimes appeared in sectarian movements, manifests the legalistic error. Protestantism not infrequently falls into the antinomian error. If what has been said about the matter of principles is valid, then it follows that casuistry must draw on both elements in the Christian heritage. It must draw

philosophies to answer the questions of faith. Apologetics in this aggressive sense gives no ground to the categories of secularism in order to make Christian faith acceptable to the secular world. Whereas in much philosophy of religion of the liberal bent secular categories had become the accepted instruments of common conversation between theologians and secular scholars, in true apologetics the working ground is decidedly Christian.

This rediscovery of a term focused tendencies that had been growing widely and robustly in the Church for many years. It gave the historic name to the reality which had been rediscovered. The Church had rediscovered the significance of Biblical faith, thus breaking with a foreign theological orientation based on the categories of humanism. The Church had rediscovered the role of Christian faith as an interpretation of human existence challenging all contending interpretations. The Church had rediscovered the given and revealed character of Christian truth — a truth not derived from the idealism of men, but based upon the living Word of God. Christianity was no longer treated by theology as the fulfillment of human ideals — as the best of man's many religions — but as saving and ultimate truth in its own right. The term apologetics has become accepted in responsible theology only because neo-orthodoxy had revived earlier and orthodox perspectives on the Bible, revealed faith, and saving truth.

Nevertheless, contemporary books on apologetics, like the book by Alan Richardson entitled *Christian Apologetics,* are meaningful to our day because they are more than a traditional rehash. They speak from the perspective of a theology that has known the concern of Christian liberalism to make Christian faith pertinent to the whole range of human learning and experience. Christian apologetics in the rediscovered sense is as distinct from the apologetics of religious conservatism as a Christian casuistry in the rediscovered sense ought to be distinct from the forces that have brought it into disrepute as a concept.

At the beginning of his work, Alan Richardson writes thus of his task:

"The aim of this Preface is to indicate the standpoint and argument of this work by setting it within the wider context of present-day thought upon the problem of the nature of our knowledge, more particularly of our scientific knowledge. Christian apologetics deals with the question of the nature and validity of our knowledge of God, and thus compels us to examine the methods and conclusions of theological inquiry in the light of our general knowledge of the world around us and of ourselves in relation to that world" (*Christian Apologetics*, p. 7. Harper & Brothers, 1947).

Such a concern to understand and appreciate the whole sweep of human knowledge in relation to Christian truth does not come from the mind-set of narrowly theological conservatism. It comes rather from a broad interest in the nature of the sciences and humanities. Such an interest is characteristic of Christian liberalism and is prompted by a desire that Christianity shall speak a pertinent word to a contemporary age. Had this urge not infused Richardson's work, his book would have been only a rehearsal of antiquated categories; as it stands, it is a restatement of historic Christian faith in relation to a new historical context.

A rediscovery of casuistry will only be futile if it comes as an attempt to reinstate unchanged an ancient scheme of casuistry. One of the errors of Roman Catholicism is to yearn for the return of culture to the Middle Ages and the return of Christian ethics to the scholastic system. Sometimes Protestantism yearns for a return to the past, to the Puritan days for example. But returns of this sort would produce the situations of antiquity, not a creative rediscovery of the historic Christian answer in the present time of need. Just as the re-use of the term "apologetics" would have proved stifling without the contributions of the very theological liberalism that had been prone to distrust the word, so the re-use of the term "casuistry" will be of little avail without the contributions of modern insights. The Christian must be ever searching for rediscovery and re-creation of ancient truths of faith in relation to the new situations of his time. He must never condone reactionary effort to revive a past *status quo*.

Rediscovery of casuistry will include an understanding of the tension between "man's disorder and God's design." The best theology of the contemporary Church understands the tension in all its naked manifestations. The Church stands in debt to a generation of thinkers who have made it aware of all the difficulties involved in obedience to Christian standards in a non-Christian world. It stands in debt to those who have led it to recognize the illusive nature of all attempts to apply Christian love to social problems without a casuistry. A generalized acceptance of the term "apologetics" (which is the thought of the Church in relation to the world) can help to win acceptance for the term "casuistry" (which is the life of the Church in relation to the world).

Important as the understanding of compromise is for the discovery of casuistry in our time, no true rediscovery of casuistry can come until there is a renewed sense of God's design working in, and passing beyond, man's disorder. The Church must come to understand this truth in all its creative implications. Christian faith is permitted no sentimental illusions about making love relevant to the world, but it is forbidden to despair of the effort. Casuistry is not just the science of compromise; it is the reasonable service of the conscience which calls Christians to express loving concern for their fellow man within the limits of social possibility. To understand this in the context of faith is to know the meaning of casuistry, and to act in accord with it in a life of devoted obedience to Christ is to affirm its validity.

THE STRUCTURE OF CASUISTRY

CHAPTER **IV**

The Gospel and Casuistry

A CHRISTIAN casuistry must loyally attempt to implement the requirements of the gospel ethic. It can have no legitimate goal except to do the will of God as revealed in Jesus Christ. God wills that men should love one another as he has loved them. Love is the norm of Christian obedience, stringent in character and absolute in demand. The love by which Christians are guided was made known through the revelation of God as perfected in Jesus Christ his Son. This Christian love is a guide to personal conduct; it is also the ultimate norm by which all concrete actions are brought under judgment. Christians serve under a compulsion so demanding that it can never be entirely fulfilled. " Greek moralists bade us avoid the ' too much.' But . . . ' nothing too much ' is no motto for the Christian, for the God he worships is the God who has met his need in the hyperbole of the cross " (Sydney Cave, *The Christian Way*, p. 165. Philosophical Library, Inc.).

A Christian neglects this truth only at his peril. God lays a total demand upon him. He is to love God with all his being. God is a holy and righteous judge, the ruler over all that men do. Christian love is no ordinary good will, but a revolutionary demand upon a person's whole being that radically challenges his normal mores. Men worry about the needs of the future; Christian faith bids them be not anxious. Men naturally hate and resist those who persecute them; Christians are told to love their enemies. Men seek to save their talents by prudence and temperance in all things; Christians are expected to devote everything they possess to the God from whom they received it. Who is so bold, yea, even so blind, as to suppose that he measures up to such requirements?

Christian love is an absolute demand because God is absolute. God is holy; he allows no competitors for the devotion of the Christian. To serve lesser gods is to fall into idolatry. To misunderstand, or simply not to understand, the all-demanding nature of God's rule is to eclipse the meaning of his holy providence and to forget that he alone is Lord. To suppose that man's devotion to God is ever completed on the basis of what man does in the way of ethical good works is to forget the gulf that exists between God's will and all human attempts to fulfill it.

Much contemporary theology has made us acutely aware of man's inability to serve God completely. Until men acknowledge the partiality of their service, especially in comparison with the absoluteness of God's will, they cannot even hope to know the meaning of the gospel message. Without this doctrine of God's utter holiness the Protestant element in Christianity is lost. Any valid Christian ethic acknowledges the majesty of God and the judgment over men that is found (together with love for them) in the selfless sacrifice of Christ. Divine love judges all human approximations of that love as well as the flagrant rejection of its truth and claim so rampant today. To understand this judgment is the first task of a Protestant ethic.

It is obvious that in the contemporary world men do not love as they were meant to love. Fighting and wars between nations, corruption and class conflicts within nations, divorce and broken relationships within families, personal feuds and small bickerings between individuals — all these witness to a condition of life in which men have long failed to treat each other as brothers in Christ. Too many men today regard their fellow men as tools and powers to be manipulated for private gain.

Divine love judges this condition; it judges each man for having a part in it. Acknowledgment of human sin in this sense is a sober insight. There can be no genuine Christianity where men do not understand their inadequacy and their involvement in sin. There can be no genuine understanding of this involvement where men do not know the demands of God's love by which human life is brought under judgment.

It is to Jesus that we must go for our initial understanding of Christian love. Absolute Christian love is to be measured only by the teaching and example of Christ, who made the claim of neighbor as great as the claim of self and the claim of God greater than both. Christian love is the unstinting love of every possible neighbor for the sake of service to God, a love that seeks its only reward in the joy of faithful obedience to God. Such a love can love even those who persecute it and can rejoice even when falsely maligned by those whom it seeks to serve. Its mood appears in the Gospel accounts, perhaps no more wistfully than in Jesus' weeping over the city of Jerusalem:

"O Jerusalem, Jerusalem, killing the prophets and stoning those who are sent to you! How often would I have gathered your children together as a hen gathers her brood under her wings, and you would not!" (Matt. 23:37, R. S. V.).

Jesus' portrayal of Christian love as a love intoxicated with the sense of duty to God is difficult to define in the categories of philosophical thought. Surely it has transcendent and absolute elements. Whenever men seek to describe these in philosophical categories, they are driven to limited formulas. Jesus' ethic of love defies abstraction, yet to some extent demands it, for just as we do not conceive of God without some use of theological ideas, so we do not conceive of the Christian ethic without generalized propositions.

One may speak of Christian love as an ultimate norm. Certainly it is greater than our human conceptions of practicality and plausible decency. One may think of this ultimacy of Christian love as a self-giving love patterned after God's activity in Christ, as Nygren does in describing *agape*. Accordingly, Paul Ramsey suggests that Christian love has no place for self-regard, but is a completely disinterested love for the neighbor. These are abstract categories attempting to describe what can only be lived. They have been accused by thinkers like Joseph Haroutunian and H. Richard Niebuhr of turning the gospel norm into a humanistic system of value perfectionism, of making the ideal of Christian love so abstractly unrealistic as to rob it of practical relevance to what men can accomplish in daily life.

Dangerous as may be the attempt to describe Christian love in perfectionistic terms, these terms can emphasize its ultimacy, and must do so. If Jesus' ethic cannot be turned into a value perfectionism, still less can it be made into a humanistic prudentialism. It is not a set of conventional virtues that risks little in being traditionally good. One can only shudder when he sees it appealed to as an equivalent of be-kind-to-animals week, as the professed guide of the merchants' association, as the kind of practical code proposed in Sheldon's famous book *In His Steps*. When a business bureau or a political club or a nation-state naïvely asserts that its activities are guided by the simple teachings of the Sermon on the Mount, one can conclude only that it understands very little of its implications. Perhaps the abstract language of the theologians is misleading, but it does guard against complacent naïveté, a naïveté too prevalent in the American church.

Christian love as found in the life and teachings of Jesus appears to be far beyond the normal definitions of love. The career of Jesus was a protest against the legalistic casuistry of Judaism and the narrow and self-regarding motives that had corrupted Pharisaism. The transcendent demands of Christian love are given greatest emphasis in those elements of Jesus' teaching aimed directly at the legalism that was perverting the real purpose of the law. At the risk of being misinterpreted one might suggest that Jesus, as a prophet rather than a responsible moralist, was not concerned to lay down a meaningful structure of lawful action but to disturb those who claimed more righteousness for an existing structure than it actually possessed. As Dr. Fosdick puts it, " Jesus presented to any self-complacent person an ethical ideal that made blamelessness impossible " (*op. cit.,* p. 94).

Those teachings of Jesus which aim to destroy the pretensions of the would-be righteous are not the whole of the gospel message. Alone, they are not a sufficient guide to the understanding of the nature of Christian love. No definition of Christian love is adequate if it emphasizes only the transcendence of God's demand. Whenever Christian ethics make love into merely a norm that judges all human actions (albeit it does have this role), it ceases to be true to the whole truth of the gospel. The gospel portrays love to us in the person of Christ. Christ is not only God but also man. His love is significant for practical human decisions. To define Christian love as though it has no possible incarnation in human activity is to make it too transcendent. Love has a creative role in the affairs of men. The gospel sets its ultimate before men in an incarnation. Thus the absolute nature of Christian love is complemented by a practical side. Casuistry is necessary in order to translate the high demands of love into relevance for the world; it is possible because love can be so translated. Divine love is creatively relevant to human situations. Compromise action, which is the action of casuistry, is ethically meaningful because it embodies as well as contradicts the ultimate norm. It is not sufficient to know the pretension and sin within all ethical action. We must also know the incarnation of the divine within the human and the creative possibility of human goodness by grace.

The teaching of our Lord brings out the creative interplay between love as a norm and love as an act. In the parable of the Good Samaritan the sin of the righteous two who pass on the other side of the road is counterbalanced by the act of the third man who expresses love for his neighbor. The elder brother in the parable of the Two Sons receives just criticism as a harsh and proud protector of his private due; the father expresses the real love of parent for child which thereby becomes the gospel prototype. In the parables rich men are judged for the use of their riches in the manipulation of fellow men toward narrow and selfish goals; but a widow quietly slips her mite into the offering. The teachings of Jesus contain both judgment upon the actions of finite men, especially when they forget their finiteness, and portrayal of simple human virtue that expresses, in the context of obedience to God, the nature of devoted love. The judgment of God upon the pretensions of the righteous is balanced by the grace of God at work in the devotion of the humble. Surely we cannot do without either emphasis.

Interpreters have not always been able to give full justice to both emphases in the teachings of Jesus. Some give too much attention to the criticism of rabbinic legalism; others, too much attention to the place of love in the humble acts of common life. Those who see the criticism of legalism as the dominant note tend to use the ethic of Jesus in its more perfectionistic sense and thus deny its significance for common decisions. Those who see how Jesus portrayed love as possible in simple acts tend to forget the difficulties involved in making love relevant to complex social decisions. Ernst Troeltsch, looking at Jesus' criticism of the Pharisees, concluded that Christ was concerned only for the final religious dimensions of an ethic. He tacitly disapproved of the way in which Jesus overlooked social problems. Troeltsch would have been pleased with less " heroic " teaching on the part of Jesus and more concern for the alleviation of material pauperism and the breaking of Palestine's yoke of oppression. Walter Rauschenbusch, impressed by the practical implications of Christ's teaching, saw in its precepts the spiritual dynamic that could establish a truly righteous social order by blasting away all dogmatic and political tyrannies. Albert Schweitzer, whose missionary career in Africa has captured the imagination of the entire world, sees the ethic of Jesus as suitable for an apocalyptic, but not for a general, situation. James Hastings Nichols, writing as a Church historian, sees in the teachings of Jesus an ethical rigorism that the Church lacked the spiritual stamina to maintain, once it sought to appease the social policies of the Constantinian empire.

This welter of conflicting interpretations shows that rather than solving the casuistic problem by criticizing the legalism of the Jews, Jesus simply re-created it. Take as an example his teaching concerning tribute to Caesar: " Render therefore to Caesar the things that are Caesar's, and to God the things that are God's " (Matt. 22:21, R. S. V.). This is a brilliant answer to a question intended to ensnare Jesus, and lays down a general principle of considerable value in analyzing the relationship of the Christian to God and to the State. But the answer cannot be taken as a blueprint for solving all the complex problems that arise between Church and State. To urge the payment of taxes does not give guidance as to the kind of tax policy Christians should support. To sanction obedience to a conscription law gives no guidance as to whether such obedience should or should not take the form of conscientious objection within the provisions of the law. The saying of Jesus doubtless gave little comfort to early Christians who suffered martyrdom for their refusal to worship the idols which Rome had manufactured. The fundamental problem of casuistry is to deal with situations in which a Caesar claims what clearly belongs to God and to resolve doubts as to what is Caesar's and what is God's in a case of conflicting claims.

Sydney Cave warns us that in relating the teachings of Jesus

to the "orders" of life — marriage, industry, and the State —
it is not possible "to win from the words of Jesus a direct answer to our modern problems" (*op. cit.,* p. 62). This is one
side of the coin; but only one side. The other side is the challenge in Christ's teaching which urges men to relate the ultimate demands which Christ has made known to the duties they
must daily perform. There are two elements in the gospel
teachings. The one is transcendent and almost makes us despair
of ever achieving such excellence in the world as it is today;
the other is homespun realism that teaches us to seek to love our
neighbors in common life.

The tension created by these elements is present not only in
the teachings of Jesus but in the whole history of Christian
common life. Paul interpreted his misery in terms of the contrast between what he knew he ought to do and what he actually
found himself doing. Paul rose to ecstatic heights of ethical devotion, yet also recognized the problems created by the persis-
tence of sin both in himself and in the world. The Christian
Church has been host to many movements, some of which have
been concerned to bring Christian love into human situations
while others have understood the judgment that Christian love
renders upon all human institutions and achievements. What
Ernst Troeltsch says about early Christianity can also be said
about the entire history of the Christian movement:

"Christianity seems to influence social life in two ways: Either,
on the one hand, it develops an idealistic anarchism and the communism of love, which combines radical indifference or hostility
toward the rest of the social order with the effort to actualize the
ideal of love in a small group; or, on the other hand, it develops
along social-conservative lines into an attitude of submission to God
and his will, so far as the world is concerned, combined with a
strong independence of an organized community which manages its
own affairs, which, as the range of influence increases, finds that it
cannot ignore secular institutions, but that it must do its utmost to

utilize them for its own purposes" (*The Social Teachings of the Christian Churches,* p. 82, Vol. I. London, George Allen & Unwin, Ltd., 1931).

The first strategy described by Troeltsch is that of Protestant sectarianism; the second attitude, that of the conservative and established churches. Sectarianism, though it has sometimes accepted a rigorous standard for a group removed from the world, has also appeared in a variety that seeks the transformation of the world itself. This attempt to create a new social order along specifically Christian lines often leads to an oversimplification of the Christian ethic and a sentimental understanding of the relationship of love to social institutions. In fairness to sectarianism it must be added that this very oversimplification has prompted a heroic Christian living of a type hardly ever present in the conservative wing of Christianity. The conservative wing, preoccupied, as it has usually been, with the sense of contrast between the majesty of God and the sinfulness of all human institutions, has frequently cut the nerve of Christian social action by failure to seek the transformation of culture into conformity with a radical understanding of Christian love.

The Roman Catholic Church is likewise subject to a tendency to apply the Christian ethic in two ways. Leaving the life of utter devotion to love for the monastic, it has sought to control the social order in accord with a minimal conception of the Christian demand as derived from natural law. The Catholic strategy goes two ways at once, dealing robustly with cultural forces on the basis of a rational ethic and providing, for those called to the monastic life, an avenue of more rigorous devotion in a protected type of living. This produces a schizophrenic tendency, dividing the church into laity and clergy with different standards for each.

Failures to hold to both dimensions of the truth in the gospel continue to mark the contemporary life of the Church. Christian love is relevant to life and its concrete demands for ethical and moral change are essential parts of Christian duty. These demands cannot be left out of Christian living without peril to its fullness. Christians must recognize the significance and the legitimacy of historical expressions of love and also the limitations and partiality of these very same expressions. God's majesty is flouted by the historical decisions of disobedient men, and the men are consequently brought under his judgment — but aspects of divine love are incarnate in human actions whenever men bring themselves into submission to the will of God in Christ. There is a place for both Luther and Wesley in Christian faith, for both the idea of judgment as expressed in " theologies of sin " and the idea of grace expressed in " theologies of hope." To break the tension between these two dimensions is to lose the essential creativity of the gospel which makes it unique as an understanding of the human situation.

The gospel demands a casuistry. The gospel is a final standard of righteousness, the ultimate framework in which judgment upon all human disobedience takes place. It is also a demand and promise for creative living. Christian faith is permitted no ethical norm aside from the gospel ethic of love. Christians are bound to the love of God and the neighbor. Human efforts to express the content of this love are always partial, but this very partiality negatively considered makes a casuistic framework necessary and positively considered makes it possible.

CHAPTER V

Casuistry and Culture

RELIGION uses both material goods and human communities in order to express itself and witness to spiritual realities. Imagine a religion without language, without art, without the paraphernalia of meetinghouse or cathedral! Such a religion might infuse the mind of an isolated mystic, but it could hardly become a social movement. Christianity finds expression in tangible and social realities that include all types of human accomplishment — the homes men create, the businesses at which they earn their bread and butter, the clubs and movie houses that furnish their recreation. It is these realities which the New Testament calls " the world " and which are today more commonly referred to as culture.

Modern men are the victims of a secular outlook which has made religion one department of life among many other departments. This state of mind generally regards the nonreligious departments of life as beyond the scope and pale of religious influence. When men divide life into sacred and secular areas of concern, they forget that religion can find expression only through cultural channels. They divorce the worship that goes on in church from the life that goes on outside the church.

To be faithful to Christ and to obey his commandment of love requires that Christians be obedient to him in all the areas of life. If the demand of Christian love is a full and unconditional demand for total obedience, then it calls for this obedience to express itself in all aspects of culture. Christians cannot escape from the world in order to perform their duties to God; in fact, duty to God can be performed only by those who seek to do his will in the world about them.

Culture furnishes the condition within which a Christian ethic must work and to which it must be relevant. The norm of Christian obedience is determined by the gospel, but the framework of its application is determined by culture. It is here that the problems begin, for while Christian love must express itself in relation to its surrounding environment, the surrounding environment does not always permit it to do so. The world is not a world in which obedience to Christ is easily expressed, in which Christian virtue is always honored, in which devotion to Christian love is assured of success. Culture furnishes the medium through which Christian love must express itself, but it also forces the compromises that are involved in relating love to human life.

Sober Christian thought has always recognized this ambivalence in the relation of Christian faith to culture. The New Testament describes Christians as in the world but not of it. Saint Paul warned his followers not to be conformed to the world in seeking to transform it. Saint Augustine spoke of the world as a place of two intermeshed cities, the earthly city of sin and self-love and the heavenly city of love for God.

Consider first how culture forces compromise of Christian standards. Augustine described the earthly city as a city "divided against itself by litigations, wars, quarrels, and such victories as are either life-destroying or short-lived " (*City of God* XV, 4). This earthly city is not of itself evil, but it leads to evil because of its self-love.

"The things which this city desires cannot justly be said to be evil, for it is itself, in its own kind, better than all other human goods. For it desires earthly peace for the sake of enjoying earthly goods, and it makes war in order to attain this peace. . . . [The inhabitants of the earthly city] neglect the better things of the heavenly city . . . and so inordinately covet these present good things that they believe them to be the only desirable things " (*ibid.*).

The conflict of interest and loyalties, both within the earthly city and between the earthly city and the heavenly city, tears the Christian conscience and forces it to compromise. For the sake of fellowship with a social club a Christian may be called upon to lower his own personal standards and act " as one of the boys." In business, where he earns the livelihood for his family, he may contradict his integrity in order to hold his job. As members of a political party men are tempted to conform to its dictates rather than to maintain their critical independence. In the effort to protect the values for which nations stand, citizens fight and slaughter fellow men in modern war.

Human society is a good creation, but it does not enjoy a simple and innocent goodness. It creates those situations which become stumbling blocks to men of faith. The world in which men live is both good and evil in its influence, but it seems to compound human sin even more readily than it compounds human virtue. In *Moral Man and Immoral Society,* Reinhold Niebuhr has pointed out that what men would never do individually they consent to do corporately, being carried along by group pressure and frenzy. What is individual selfishness becomes group injustice; what is personal cantankerousness breeds social war. Cultural groupings produce class divisions, economic injustices on an exploitive scale, patterns of organized segregation, and military conflicts.

The culture that surrounds Christians embodies a consolidated order of sin. Christians are usually involved in the sin of their social group, and the institutional Church compounds it with evils of its own making. But Christians are called to acknowledge their sin and to overcome it; they are to seek to be obedient to Christ in a largely disobedient world. This world, even where it is nominally Christian, includes vitalities and forces seeking to destroy Christian values. To deal with the realities that confront them in this situation Christians need a casuistry. Christians can express their devotion to love only partially in culture. Frequently this partial expression of love calls for seeming contradictions. Only by withdrawal from the orders of human society can compromises with society be completely avoided.

The Christian movement painfully learned this fact about its relation to culture in the transition it made from its status before the time of Constantine to its status as the official religion of the Empire. The Early Church, persecuted by the Roman State, took no active role in political or social life. Ernst Troeltsch criticized this failure on the part of early Christianity to meet the problems of its surrounding culture. Troeltsch regarded early Christianity as purely religious, and was concerned over its failure to deal with the social implications of its ethical insight. Specifically, he condemned the failure of the early Christian society to challenge the institution of slavery, to develop interest in economic justice, to reach a social outlook in the place of gnostic mysticism. " The possibility," he said, ". . . of using the ordinances of Society positively . . . lies still entirely beyond the vision of the Early Church " (*op. cit.,* pp. 82 f.).

The pre-Constantinian Church, however, had maintained an ethical rigorism that was lost as soon as the Church was officially recognized by the Empire. James Hastings Nichols comments regarding this development:

" Early in the fourth century occurred the most far-reaching change in the status and character of Christianity since the days of Paul. The pagan emperor Constantine, whether from superstitious fear or from calculations of expediency, reversed the policy of persecution and sought to use Christianity as a cohesive bond in his disintegrating empire. For three centuries Christians had been segregated in the Empire as Negroes are in the modern United States. Periodically they had endured lynching, and, toward the end, State attempts at complete suppression. Their business, recreation, and personal relations had been to a remarkable degree confined to their own fellowship and their moral standards were conspicuously higher than those of the society about them. They had made no serious effort to master and transform the pagan civilization about them, but had lived apart, nonpolitical and predominantly pacifist, a suffering minority. But now with the Constantinian revolution this high visibility of the Christian fellowship became obscured, and, as has been the case with the Church in Western civilization ever since in large measure, it became hard to tell Christian from non-Christian on a working day. . . . It would be the radical separatists of the Reformation who would first recapture the full earnestness of the martyr spirit and the holy remnant of the pre-Constantinian Church " (*Primer for Protestants,* pp. 28 f. Association Press, 1947).

There is no gainsaying this contention that Constantine's acceptance of the Church and the Church's acceptance of a relationship to the Empire were detrimental to a rigorous adherence to the standards of the gospel. In the historical changes that accompanied the official recognition of the Christian religion and its consequent assimilation into the main stream of culture one value was traded for another. The shift of the Early Church, from the persecuted minority that was set against culture into the official religion of the culture, resulted in a gain of status and influence but a loss of that heroic and saintly devotion characteristic of the early martyrs.

The Constantinian revolution highlighted the basic relationship between gospel and culture. Gospel and culture exist in tension. This tension has always prevented an entirely satisfactory relation between the Christian faith and its surrounding society. Monasticism and radical separatism have tended to withdraw from culture for the sake of rigorous allegiance to the gospel ethic; conservative and established Christianity, to compromise the rigor of the gospel in order to identify itself with the main stream of culture. Christianity tends to be rigoristic in rough proportion to its withdrawal from responsibility for existing social orders and to compromise its ideals whenever it takes major institutional responsibility for existing political and social arrangements.

The history of Christian social life is not without attempted exceptions to this rule. Certainly Calvin thought his Geneva to be such an exception, and the recent social gospel firmly hoped to Christianize the social order as a whole. Moreover, as H. Richard Niebuhr has so carefully shown us in *Christ and Culture,* five, rather than merely two, predominant patterns characterize the relationship of the Church and its environment. And yet, in sketching the enduring nature of the problem, Niebuhr notes that " not only pagans who have rejected Christ, but believers who have accepted him, find it difficult to combine his claims upon them with those of their societies " (p. 10. Harper & Brothers, 1951).

Culture forces the compromises with which the casuistic process must reckon as it aids the Christian in making his faith relevant to society. Culture is a downward pull working against the upward pull of the gospel. The tensions between the gospel and culture make a casuistry of some sort inevitable. No complete following of the ethical admonitions of Christ is ever culturally possible, for Christ's demands always stand above the conditions of culture.

If this constituted the whole story, then the strategy of Christians would be relatively simple. They would be called to withdraw from culture in order to preserve a rigorous ethic. They would attempt to preserve the purity of faith free from the blemishes of the world. Withdrawal, demanding as it would be of high ethical devotion, would comprise a simple solution as compared to the tortuous path involved in casuistry.

Christians cannot simply withdraw from culture because culture is more than the source of compromise: it is a medium for expressing Christian values. It is ambiguous, as often a vehicle of positive Christian purpose as its contradiction. Christian love is driven to culture — at least a culture of some sort — in order to express itself in concrete terms. For instance, culture alone gives specific form to the ideal of community, which aside from social institutions is nothing but an abstraction. If love for neighbor is attempted apart from having a neighbor, then love of neighbor is merely a figment of the imagination. What Nels Ferré calls " true society " comes to fruition in " actual society," even though they can never be equated.

Orthodox and conservative Christianity is true to an important element in Christian faith when it concerns itself with the social structures that surround it. All protests against Roman Catholic asceticism and sectarian withdrawal are valid protests. They are valid because they understand that Christian faith cannot complete itself apart from involvement in society at large.

Christians can work in culture because it can embody Christian ends as well as contradict them. Culture belongs to the order of creation, which, though crisscrossed with sin, is ultimately in the service of God and is not merely opposed to his will. It is the creative hope in this truth that drives Christian ethics to intercourse with society and culture, even though the sin in culture causes the gospel to be compromised at the point where it meets the culture.

In relating themselves to culture, Christians will depend to some extent upon secular social analysis. They may be tempted to take a particular analysis as valid, forgetting that culture's own self-understanding is not static. Philosophies of culture change and sociological analysis varies. In this century two quite different views of culture and society have dominated the scene. One of these views, stemming from the Enlightenment and coming to fruition in modern humanitarianism, has looked upon social organization as a product of cohesive social unity, and justice as the creative achievement of constitutional law. With this stream of thought have been identified doctrines like the Social Contract theory of society and belief in human progress. This view emphasizes the capacity of cultural institutions to express community and to effect brotherhood. It is true to one facet of a Christian understanding and for plausible reasons became the sociological analysis most favored by the liberal, or social gospel, tradition. The other view dominant in this century represents a reaction against the general optimism of the Enlightenment and has reached its zenith in a Marxist ideology which sees all social relationships in terms of struggle. With this stream of thought have gone doctrines like the theory of class conflict and the inevitable clash of economic interest. This sociological analysis is far more pessimistic than the liberal one and tends to regard social justice as a product of a social struggle between classes. It generally regards power as the only realistic means of dealing with power or of changing political reality. Because this analysis has affinities with the Christian understanding of society as an order of sinful self-interests, it logically was incorporated into much neo-orthodox thought.

Both these analyses of social dynamics are products of culture's own self-appraisal and are not clearly drawn deductions from Christian ultimates. They are both legitimate tools of Christian social thought unless they are taken as final rather than provisional judgments. The humanitarian view, when taken as the whole truth about society, leads to an oversimplification of the problem of relating love to any social order. The opposite view, when taken as the whole truth, tends to underestimate the place of love in changing social relationships. Christianity, bearing witness to the role of culture both as an order of sin and as an order of grace, will accept the contributions of both these views without confusing itself with either. When fused with an optimistic Enlightenment view of culture, the gospel can be a sentimentality; when fused with the opposite view, it can be a source of despair regarding the possibilities of creative achievement. To be sober, yet hopeful in all things, requires a balance between the two extremes that have made their way into our thinking about society.

Culture changes; it changes in both the manner in which it forces ethical compromise for those who bear allegiance to Christ and also in the ways it enables them to give concrete embodiment to Christian ideals. No returns to past cultural situations are possible. Casuistry must work in the conditions of this time and be flexible enough to meet new developments. A serious error tempting Roman Catholicism is the yearning for a perpetuation of medieval culture, as though it is the only possible basis of Christian civilization. Casuistry must be open and fluid and responsive to new cultural situations; it cannot be hardened into a rigid legalism, attempting to define Christian obligation forever.

Casuistry is the meeting ground of Christian love and cultural necessity. It works out such concrete expressions of the ultimate principle of Christian love as are feasible within, and meaningful to, a given culture. Christian faith has always had the equivalent of a casuistry and has manifested a great variety of ways for relating the gospel to culture. We pause in the two succeeding chapters to examine critically both conscious and unconscious attempts at this process.

CHAPTER **VI**

Concealed Forms of Casuistry

CHRISTIANS do not always recognize the compromises they make in adjusting to the world about them. Many of them are unaware of the necessity of a casuistry and others cannot even be convinced that a tension exists between the demands of Christian love and the decisions they are daily required to render. Here is a businessman who sees no basic conflict between the radical demands of a Christian love that would serve the needy neighbor and the necessities of making private gain; here is a politician who sees no conflict between the manipulation of power (provided it is done with conventionally " clean " methods) and the Christian judgment over all power wielded for the sake of self-interest; here is a preacher (sometimes the most consummate problem of all) who sees no basic conflict between Christian faith and individual showmanship or ecclesiastical stair-climbing. The allegiance of these people to Christian ideals cannot be questioned; their desire to act as Christians is beyond dispute. Their error does not consist of going into business, into politics, or into the ministry — not even of making the compromises of ultimate Christian standards necessary to succeed in these fields. It consists rather in a failure to acknowledge the type of compromise into which they have been forced and in a failure to deal with the compromise in conscious recognition of its dangers.

Christians cannot escape an adjustment of their faith, with all its high demands, to the world of harsh realities that surrounds them. If they ignore or reject the conscious problem of casuistry, they do not escape the problem; they merely recast it. They develop a casuistry of default, reaching an adjustment of norms and actions without being aware of the compromise in the process. Many people who suppose themselves obedient to Christ have not the slightest inkling that the world in which they live, and their method of living in it, is a far step from what obedience to the Master really entails.

Casuistry by default plays a large role in the Christian community, for it characterizes large portions of the Church which identify the gospel with local customs and parochial traditions. Groups who reach an adjustment between the demands of the gospel and the conditions of culture without understanding the radical nature of the gospel or the perverse nature of their culture frequently commit gross evil in the name of the Church. They lay the Church open to the charge of hypocrisy, of not practicing what it preaches, of failing to be true to its Lord. This concealed form of casuistry is one way of adjusting faith and conduct. It is widespread in the contemporary Church.

Casuistry is an inevitable reality in Christian life; it will take unconscious forms if not permitted free and acknowledged expression. Perhaps we ought to reserve the term " casuistry " for strategies that consciously meet the problem of compromise and more fully understand the agonized involvements of their action. But it is not necessary thus to limit the term. To call a concealed and unconscious adjustment of norm and conduct a casuistry is to speak in the same sense as to call atheism a type of faith or agnosticism a variety of religious outlook.

The casuistry of an unrecognized compromise was present in an embryonic form in the period just following the Constantinian revolution, but it has become more common in the modern Church. For a few years following Constantine the Church was a stranger in a cultural tradition shaped by paganism, trying to identify its life with that of secular power and authority.

But this situation did not last long, for the Church soon became mother of the culture. This involved compromise, to be sure, as any student of the Middle Ages can quickly verify; but this compromise tended to express itself in conscious forms of casuistry. The Early Church withdrew from the pagan culture in a rigoristic attempt to preserve the purity of its own ethic. The medieval Church, however, dominated its culture in the effort to make it conform to minimal " Christian " standards. Its compromise was with itself rather than with an external world. The modern Church, due to forces beyond its making or control, has been thrown into a secular world. It lives much as did that Constantinian Church, a tacitly accepted element in a cultural world largely indifferent, if not antagonistic, to the Christian faith. Thus the modern Church has been most clearly tempted to unrecognized compromise. It, in particular, has been tempted by purely secular pressures impinging upon it from a culture that it has long ceased effectively to shape. It lives in a secular world whose concerns and interests are too often those of what Richard Kroner calls the " post-Christian era."

The danger to which the modern Church has become exposed is the more acute because the secularized world is not clearly recognized for what it is — a secularized world. Too many people tacitly assume that contemporary culture is Christian culture, both in name and actuality. They have not understood the loss (as well as the gain) that came with the breakdown of the Church authority of the Middle Ages. Modern man acknowledges no transcendent or overarching authority. Each of the disciplines of modern life claims unfettered freedom to pursue its own ends; each sovereign State refuses to submit to any overarching norm. No clearer illustration of this bankruptcy can be cited than in the case of the conduct of war. In the Middle Ages the authority of the Church was of sufficient strength to enforce the so-called truce of God, preventing private war on Friday, Saturday, and Sunday of every week. In our century of total war such a truce would be impossible even to hope for. In fact, modern war has now become so total that even the humanitarian principles that as late as World War I were held inviolate have all but evaporated. The freedom of medical contingents to pursue their acts of mercy as noncombatants, the fair treatment of prisoners, and other principles designed to alleviate the awful necessities of combat — all these are going by the board in a world that seems to honor no principles of decency at all. In fact, the problem of casuistry can be no more vividly illustrated in general humanitarian terms than at this point. How is a democratic West, fighting to preserve the principles of decency, to combat a ruthless foe which does not honor them? If the West holds too many scruples, it may lose the combat; if it sells out its scruples, it has succumbed to the ways of the enemy.

The modern Church must seek to live in a culture that has long since ceased to bear allegiance to Christian standards, except nominally perhaps. Modern culture has grown secular through a series of developments over which the Church has been able to exercise little control. Each secular department of life has declared its independence from Christian authority, often for justifiable reasons explained by the Church's own misuse of the authority it once enjoyed. This development is described in the intellectual realm by Paul Tillich as follows:

" The triumph of autonomous knowledge, particularly in the natural sciences, has pushed aside religious knowledge. Either it is repudiated altogether or it is relegated to a corner, or it is transformed by secular interpretations. The last fate is the most disastrous just because it appears to preserve the whole body of Christian truth. In reality it alters the meaning of all beliefs. It makes them a phase of secular knowledge . . ." (" The World Situation," in *The Christian Answer,* Henry P. Van Dusen, editor, p. 37. Charles Scribner's Sons, 1945).

The transformation of religious knowledge by secular interpretations has its counterpart in the realm of ethics. Christian ethics has been transformed into the general humanitarianism of Western culture. This humanitarianism is of itself a value to be prized, but it is not the summation of Christian virtue. It is a secularized idealism that for plausible reasons gets called " Christian " when the radical demands of the gospel have been forgotten.

The relegation of religious knowledge to the corner of which Tillich speaks also has its counterpart in the realm of ethics. Christian concerns have been replaced by a host of lesser loyalties that are basically secular in character. The growth of autonomous disciplines in the modern era has made possible a set of secular alternatives to the Christian faith. These in turn make for a default casuistry of unrecognized compromise such as marks the contemporary Church in alarming measure. The process of unrecognized compromise is serious at the present time because the cultural pattern is less and less congenial to Christian faith. The very forces that have made for autonomy in ethics have also made for autonomy in politics, with the resulting growth of absolutized patriotism. Likewise, these forces have driven toward autonomy in economic life, with tendencies to allow business to set its own codes of behavior quite apart from basic religious considerations.

Far from being the object of Christian judgment, these developments have become the channels of so-called " Christian " virtue in the eyes of many people. For example, the radical tension between Christian faith and jingoistic patriotism has been all but lost. The position of the American flag in many churches is a matter of greater concern to the people than any problem relating to specifically religious issues. In many communities theological concerns hardly stir a ripple (except in ultraconservative groups notorious for intolerance), but let someone in our culture, even in the church, refuse to conform to some patriotic symbolism, and the entire community's wrath is apt to be visited upon him. Indeed, the participation of the average churchman in the war effort of his nation is seldom prompted by a theologically orientated understanding as to the justification for such action in a Christian ethic, but by unqualified allegiance to the State. How different from the Middle Ages, in which no Christian would have considered performing any service to the State except in expression of his Christian loyalty!

Likewise, Christians have all but forgotten the tension between the gospel ethic and inordinate degrees of success in the modern commercial world. When Jesus instructed his disciples to take no thought for the morrow or asked the rich young ruler to sell all his possessions and give the benefits to the poor, he rendered a harsh judgment upon pinch-penny planning and privately hoarded wealth. Surely there ought to be a Christian uneasiness about a process that relies upon selfish gain as its basic appeal. This is not necessarily to say that no casuistic grounds justifying the profit motive are possible — the competitive market may indeed be a satisfactory way of dealing with economic life in many situations — but it is to suggest that Christian virtue can never be measured in terms of money success. In fact, one may go farther and criticize the tacit assumption all too prevalent in middle-class churches that privately accumulated, carefully saved, and piously philanthropized fortunes are a mark of Christian earnestness. The New Testament does not altogether preclude a rich man's entry into the Kingdom of Heaven, but it does suggest that he may need to do some special explaining to get in, explaining as to the grounds on which he enjoys his riches in a world of indescribable need.

Confusion of secular standards with Christian " virtue" is by no means confined to American culture. It may be worse in America because of the confusions that make it idolatrous and blur the contrast. But the Church in many cultures is likewise tempted to identify the particular social policies of its own nation with the will of God. In fact, pressures in collectivist states are even stronger, and the chances for prophetic protest even less, than is true in a free society. The fact that Martin Niemoeller's resistance to Nazism took form only after Hitler had begun to challenge the inner citadel of theological concern shows that a strategy of unrecognized compromise can be operative even in the case of one whose will to resistance for the sake of conviction cannot be questioned. It never occurred to Niemoeller that Germany's social policies under Hitler could not be condoned by a Christian as social policies of the State.

To speak as we have about the matter of patriotism and economic policy is to open ourselves to misinterpretation. It is to appear disloyal, in the eyes of some, to the values of our culture. This meaning is not intended, and the fact that it will so appear to some is a further evidence to prove the point we are seeking to drive home. Loyalty to nation and to the positive values in a democratic capitalist society are important loyalties, but to the Christian they are secondary loyalties subservient to his primary obedience to Christ. People duped by Communism make absolute their allegiance to a State and to an economic ideology. They set a new secular allegiance against their former allegiance, replacing one human system with another. Thus they are traitors in very fact, victims of a new and more terrible secularism. This new secularism does not recognize its proximate character, but makes an absolute claim of loyalty which is idolatrous and evil by every measure. For Christians any allegiance to it is categorically ruled out and resistance constantly demanded.

Christians must question the claim of any culture that does not recognize the final allegiance of men to God. If a nation, even the best of nations, demands of men a loyalty to itself above loyalty to God, then its claim must be questioned. The heritage of America has always remembered this, and because of it we have preserved our freedom of conscience and of liberty. If ever we forget as a nation that men owe primary allegiance to God and require of them blinded devotion to the state, we shall be doomed — doomed by that very confusion of proximate with ultimate loyalties which makes Communism such a menace. A democracy will tolerate religious devotion to God's absolute demands, but a dictatorship can never do so. For this reason Christians will seek to preserve democratic freedom; they will resist dictatorships as they alone have exhibited moral courage to do in recent history.

Unrecognized compromise with the ways of culture is often abetted by, or leads to, a more serious error of redefining the Christian standard. In this error, actual contradictions of Christian love that appear culturally desirable are sanctioned by religion, usually by use of the proof-text method. Instances of this are painfully easy to find. The medieval Crusades were justified in all their fury by appeal to religious motives. Slavery was sanctioned and defended by the Church for many centuries. A reactionary element in the Church of South Africa is presently defending both a dated and corrupt principle of white supremacy by use of " verbally inspired " texts.

The redefinition of the norm by which actual contradictions of love are given religious sanction is an abortive rather than a default casuistry. It is a perverse means of relating Christian faith to concrete ethical judgments. Usually a cultural " sellout " in the form of unrecognized compromise precedes the theological " sellout " of the redefined norm. The theological corruption may be the rationalization of the cultural behavior, more serious than the compromise because it adds heresy to idolatry, because it is conscious and premeditated rather than subconscious and accidental.

Whenever theological confusion reaches the point where it thus pretentiously and arrogantly justifies injustice, it is eventually challenged and cut down by creative secular forces as well as by dynamic criticism from within the Church itself. Secular idealism is often the seedbed of judgment upon religious error. The "grace" of Babylon not infrequently condemns the apostasy of Israel, a fact recognized by the prophets as they sought to bring Israel back to the true God — back from its connection with fertility deities and alien gods to allegiance to the law of Moses and the God of its fathers. The apostasy of Israel in conforming to the mores of the Canaanites is little different in degree or kind from the identities that the Church of Christ has often worked out with surrounding cultures. Like Israel, which was chastised by the wrath of its neighbors for the sin of its soul, an apostate Church suffers under the hands of its critics for the failures in its virtue.

But the protest against the corruption in the established Church also comes from within the faith itself. It comes in the form of radical sectarian protest, which is prophetic and absolutist in flavor rather than casuistic, and ethical rather than theological in its motivating urges. Sectarian rigorism in Christian ethics usually arises in sharp and radical opposition to the tendency of the Church to sell out to cultural pressures. Its role in Christian ethics cannot be underestimated or omitted save at the peril of those ethics. Sectarianism protests all the complacent compromise in orthodoxy's strategies, be the orthodoxy Roman or Protestant, the form of the evil papal corruption or suppression of the Peasants' Revolt.

But this very sectarian rigorism often develops a third form of unsatisfactory casuistry which is unconscious in the sense that it too fails to see the application of Christian ethics in casuistic terms. Rigorism withdraws from the surrounding society and fails to concern itself with the main stream of culture — seeking to escape the problem of compromise by avoiding the necessity for it. At other times sectarianism seeks to transform the world (or the worldly Church) by getting back to New Testament ethical purity. In this case the movement is valid in zeal and impetus but unsound in its social analysis and usually unsuccessful in its main enterprise. While culture is always open to proximate transformations which may at a given period be necessary, possible, and desirable, society does not lend itself to wholesale transformations that completely eliminate the contradictions of Christian love found in the body politic.

Many groups tend to be radical in limited areas. The Diggers of England were radical with regard to economic reform; the Anabaptists of the Continent, with regard to the prohibitions of oaths and distrust of government; the Quakers, particularly, with respect to participation in armed violence. Selective rigorism of this type, finding itself able to witness to only a segment of the Christian demand, is evidence of the fact that society is not given to wholesale transformation. It is also evidence of an unconscious casuistry, the choosing of a special area of conduct for rigorous treatment coupled to complete disregard of other areas.

A slightly different form of selective rigorism occurs in established Christianity whenever it makes petty personal morality the limit of its ethical concern. By providing a set of strict, though fulfillable, rules for the area of personal morality, it leaves weightier matters of ethical concern outside its purview. By concentrating on the " petty vices " it ends up negligent in the matter of social morality and political responsibility.

Such, then, are the unconscious ways in which men avoid the conscious use of a casuistry. These strategies are difficult to defend, either theologically or sociologically. They are most dangerous when they corrupt Christian faith by fitting it to cultural mores and conditions without recognizing their action; they are equally unsatisfactory when they seek to avoid compromise by withdrawal from society. Indeed, we must look beyond unconscious casuistries for an adequate way to relate the ultimate requirements of Christian love to the practical issues of life.

CHAPTER VII

Consciously Recognized Casuistries

CONCEALED or unconscious forms of casuistry tend to be dangerous because they fail to acknowledge the compromise involved in relating the Christian ethical imperative to concrete social problems. Their error springs from a failure to understand the ambiguity in all Christian action and consists of either equating proximate decisions with Christianity itself or seeking to escape from ambiguous decisions altogether.

It is plausible to expect that strategies that recognize the necessity of casuistry and openly face the difficulties will bear better fruit. Strategies that take account of the problem of compromise and the presence of ambiguity in human decisions tend to be more legitimate expressions of Christian action than those taking no account of the difficulties. However, merely to recognize the problem does not solve it. Even though inadequacy and perversion in Christian strategy are almost sure to follow a failure to recognize the casuistic problem, immunity from these faults is not necessarily guaranteed by recognition of the need for casuistry. There are both good and bad, adequate and inadequate, strategies within the area of conscious casuistry. Our task here is not only to review them but to delineate the legitimate from the illegitimate forms.

Overt casuistry is nowhere more apparent than in the life of the Roman Catholic Church, which has never lacked the capacity to create conscious strategies for dealing with the gulf between the ideals of faith and the harsh realities of the temporal order. Contemporary Roman Catholic strategy is a combination of many types of action. It includes reliance upon the double standard that sets up different requirements of virtue for clergy and laity. Lay members of the Church follow a reasonable Christian morality suitable to the conditions of life in this world; a more select clergy follow the so-called " counsels of the gospel," which call for poverty, chastity, and the renunciation of the world. The one group does the less-than-perfect work by which life in a sinful world is perpetuated and maintained; the other group follows the rigorous requirements of monastic living — requirements possible only to souls with extraordinary devotion and privileged release from the more normal problems of maintaining earthly existence.

The strategy of the double standard is a practical form of casuistry. It enables the same institution to deal with the world on a shrewdly practical level, also to witness to norms and standards of faith far above the realities of the world. The double system of Catholicism works out a relationship between the counsels of perfection and everyday living by maintaining a split personality in the same institution. The Roman Church defends this on the grounds that, as a corporate group united as the body of Christ, it is able to do what no individual can of himself do — maintain a witness to both the transcendent role of gospel standards and the practical role of everyday living.

There is a shrewdness within this system that cannot easily be denied, but it must finally be rejected, not only for its dualism but for the way in which it defines the gospel ideal. The gospel is not a call to withdrawal from the world, and when this withdrawal is motivated by personal desire for a special order of righteousness, Christian love changes from that of concern for the neighbor to a self-regard. Monasticism, despite its works of charity, its educational services, and its intercessory prayers for those who are in the world, is too open to the danger of self-seeking to constitute a very safe part of casuistry.

Moreover, the Roman double standard, by freeing the laity of the more stringent demands of love, tends to make them second-class citizens of the Church, free to conform and coerce the orders of the external world without worry as to the more ultimate compulsions of love. Thus, while the double standard of Catholicism sets up a means to express ultimate and proximate levels of Christian decision, it places each in a separate channel and fails to bring the judgment of love upon all men in the same manner.

The concept of natural law plays a somewhat more satisfactory role in Catholic morality. Natural law is a law for everyday living. It is a law of minimal and supposedly rational standards suited to the exercise of elementary Christian virtue in the common situations of life. It enables the moralist to determine what courses of action are legitimate for the Christian conscience operating in the ambiguous area of normal living. It defines a workable, reachable, standard for Christian virtue on a mundane level. A system of natural law is powerful in its effect because of the structural certainty it gives amid the ambiguities of life. With the use of natural law the Roman Catholic Church is able to define proper attitudes on most of the perplexing problems of ethical living with a categorical certainty that defies the imagination of more sensitive observers. It knows exactly what to do in the matter of birth control. It knows exactly how a decision ought to be made in cases involving choice between the life of the mother and the life of a new baby. It knows how to distinguish a just from an unjust war on the basis of clear and measurable criteria. This very certainty, however, is the source of the Roman Church's greatest temptation and final error. It leads Catholic thought to absolutize relative decisions into hard-bound legalisms. Natural law generally becomes a doctrinaire and legalistic alternative to genuine casuistry instead of a means to relate Christian judgment to concrete problems.

The requirements of love are never to be arbitrarily confined to a rational sphere of preconceived categories but are everywhere operative and unreservedly demanding. The claim of love is absolute, and every system of rational morality that fails to acknowledge this fact is subject to idolatry. Nevertheless, love of itself must set guides and norms. As Paul Ramsey points out, " love, far from being directionless, lays down its own directions, internal self-regulations conformable only to the needs of neighbor " (*Basic Christian Ethics,* p. 78. Charles Scribner's Sons, 1950). If a concept of law can be developed that will be regarded as the formulated, yet flexible, statement of the practical requirements of love in the normal situations of life, then perhaps it can contribute to casuistic guidance. Law must never be absolute; love must never be formless. The first is legalism; the second, license.

Protestantism, no less than Roman Catholicism, has developed forms of conscious casuistry. Many of these forms have been articulated by those theological orientations which have sought to deal with social problems in a time of great social turmoil. It is particularly in this type of situation that the compromise facing the Christian conscience becomes apparent, and the agony of the conscience is made real.

The casuistic framework of recent Protestant thought tends to be a dualism, varying greatly from interpreter to interpreter but well marked in its different appearances. This dualism has roots in the Augustinian-Lutheran tradition of Christian theology. In it, justice is set in contrast to love or in dialectical tension with it. Love is regarded as the ultimate principle; justice, as the practical principle for dealing with the conflicting claims found in situations of power. Emil Brunner throws these two norms into sharp antithesis. For him love is confined to personal situations; justice is the only norm for the orders of society. " The man of love can only serve the state with justice," he writes (*Justice and the Social Order,* p. 129. Harper & Brothers,

1945), implying that a Christian has two approaches toward his duty: the approach of love for situations lacking complex or coercive elements; the approach of justice for situations that are complex and political in character.

The dualism that is obvious in the thought of Brunner is more covert in the case of Reinhold Niebuhr. Niebuhr is a more prophetic and subtle thinker and holds love and justice in continual tension. Love is the ultimate, the " impossible possibility "; justice, the proximate expression of love as it weighs conflicting claims in the social order. There is always a danger that Niebuhr's formulation will become like Brunner's — making justice alone the norm for dealing with social problems and slipping love aside as an impossible norm. Justice can become the sole criterion of judgment for situations of power whenever love is considered unable to deal with the harsh realities within them. In this case justice becomes a substitute norm in place of love rather than a proximate expression of that love. The contrast between love and justice is a legitimate casuistry when set up as a tension between ultimate and proximate categories. It is false when it turns into a dualistic rather than a dialectical relationship between them.

Roman Catholic casuistry is tempted to a rigidity that expresses itself in the legalism of natural law. An opposite temptation threatens much Protestant thought, particularly that branch of Protestant thinking tempered by the philosophy and literature of existentialism. " Decisions of faith " tend to predominate this branch of Protestantism. The content of these decisions is regarded as entirely flexible and all discussion of normal Christian behavior as beside the point. It says: " Nothing is in itself good and nothing in itself bad. It all depends upon the spirit in which it is done " (Heinrich Rohrbach, " The Problem of Christian Illegal Resistance," in *The Union Seminary Quarterly Review,* June, 1952, p. 20).

Protestantism seeks to preserve the liberty of the individual

Christian conscience. It tends to distrust all legalistic moral teaching by theological authorities. It may consequently deny the need for making definitions of commonly accepted Christian behavior. In so far as Protestantism is an antidote for the overly certain attitude of the advocates of natural law and serves as a protest against these certainties, it has a crucial role to play in Christian thought. In so far, however, as it denies any possibility of defining Christian behavior in terms of ethical distinctions between right and wrong, it fades into ethical relativism akin to the secular type now poisoning Western culture.

Natural law theory is all too sure that some things are intrinsically right and others intrinsically wrong; the existential attitude of immediate decision is not sure enough. The existentialist attitude, understanding the perplexity of the Christian conscience seeking to relate Christian faith to actual life, is tempted to regard all decisions as relative in character. However, there is no logical carry-over from perplexity to relativity. The Christian conscience can never act except in the faithful hope that its decision is right, but it does not have the license to regard all decisions as of equal validity. The secular world may embrace a doctrine of ethical relativity because it has experienced a breakdown of certainty in the face of perplexity, but no such path is permitted the Christian. He may admit that every concrete choice is between shades of gray, but he can never say that the differences between the alternatives do not matter or cannot be weighed against the standard of Christian love.

Casuistry must not, as legalism does, fail to take account of the ambiguities and uncertainties that attend all human efforts to do God's will. Neither must it, as ethical relativism does, fail to take account of the decisive quality of God's revelation of the nature of love. Perhaps there is no more helpful concept for holding to both sides of this tension than that of the " middle axiom," which is a statement of goals that Christians ought specifically to strive for in a particular social situation. J. H. Oldham has said:

" As between purely general statements of the ethical demands of the gospel and the decisions that have to be made in concrete situations, there is need for what may be described as middle axioms. It is these that give relevance and point to the Christian ethic. They are attempts to define the directions in which, in a particular state of society, Christian faith must express itself. They are not binding for all time, but are provisional definitions of the type of behavior required of Christians at a given period and in given circumstances " (W. A. Visser 't Hooft and J. H. Oldham, *The Church and Its Function in Society,* pp. 193 f. Willett, Clark & Company, 1937).

A middle axiom provides both a structural element and a sense of relevance to immediate situations. As John Bennett says, " a ' middle axiom ' is more concrete than a universal ethical principle and less specific than a program that includes legislation and political strategy " (*Christian Ethics and Social Policy,* p. 77. Charles Scribner's Sons, 1946). Here is an approach that sets definable goals that draw society beyond itself without setting goals that are irrelevant to society.

Middle axioms must not be confused with Christian ultimates; neither must they be equated with calculations of expediency. They ought to enunciate goals higher than the practices of the current culture, but somewhat less demanding than the pure form of Christian love. For example, in the field of race relations Christian love would demand complete brotherhood. A middle axiom in this area, delineating a more immediate goal for which Christians ought to strive, would urge the end of legally enforced and artificially perpetuated systems of segregation. In the field of economics the ultimate norm of Christian love would urge every man to share his goods with his neighbor. A middle axiom in this area, taking into account the complex factors of incentives and property rights, would urge the elimination of involuntary pauperism within an economy of plenty. In the field of international relationships the ultimate of Christian love would demand a breakdown of all barriers between the nations. A middle axiom might set as its goal carefully supervised disarmament, leaving no nation overwhelmingly superior and no nation defenseless against unprovoked attack.

Middle axioms run the risk of being too generalized to serve as a casuistry. They may not help a man to decide how he personally can help to end segregation, to end involuntary pauperism, to help to secure supervised disarmament between the nations. They do not state what sacrifices of present values may be justified in securing new values. Nevertheless, a much fuller use of middle axioms is well in order for the Church. A clear and common mind within the Christian community is needed on the social problems of our time and it alone would do much to help Christians to work to solve these problems. If the Church is to capture the imagination of its members, guiding them in daily Christian living rather than simply leading them in a single hour of worship once a week, it must spell out middle axioms, or their equivalent, and then sustain men in the effort to implement these axioms through all that they do as members of society.

CHAPTER **VIII**

The Dialectics of Casuistry

CHRISTIANS must bear allegiance to the way of the gospel in circumstances of life permitting only partial and inadequate expressions of love. Their service to Christ always involves compromise — the compromise that results from inability to act in full accord with the demands of love and not from a disloyalty to its claim. Thus, casuistry is a dialectical process; it acknowledges a tension between a set of values above the world and a set of values in the world, both holding claim upon the conscience of the Christian.

The principles of casuistry come in pairs and can be applied only as warnings against falling into error on opposite extremes. We must engage in casuistry much as the mariners of old were forced to sail between Scylla and Charybdis. This is not to search for a golden mean, like the rational balance advocated by Aristotle. A mean strikes an average which is supposedly better than either of its components; a dialectical process maintains an uneasy tension between two contrasting values. Casuistry is not a complacent enterprise of rational harmony but a soul-taxing enterprise of ethical striving undertaken as an expression of religious faith.

The attempt to relate the demands of Christian obedience to the conditions of social culture can never be a complacent or an easy task. Bishop Stephen Neill describes the uneasy relationship of the Church to the world about it in his book *The Christian Society*. In many ways this chapter is but an exegesis of his passage:

" The Christian society can live only in a state of constant tension with its environment. In order to be itself, it must withdraw into itself, and realize its vocation to be a society governed by laws entirely different from those of its secular environment. Yet it must perpetually enter into that environment, in order that through it the world may be saved. Without that utter self-identification of sympathy and self-giving by which the incarnation was marked, it cannot be effective as the redeeming society. But if that identification goes beyond the limits marked out by its essential difference, the Christian society makes too successful an adjustment to the alien world, and loses its capacity to serve as salt and light. As long as it is in the world, it cannot but be judge of the world. The more true it is to itself, and the sterner its condemnation of all that is contrary to the will of God, the more certain it becomes that its lot will be hostility, misunderstanding, and persecution. But it is all too easy for the prophetic attitude of judgment to pass into a shrewish discontent, in which any opposition to the Church and any infringement of its privileges is identified with rebellion against God, and the defense of its *status quo* is identified with righteousness " (p. 321. Harper & Brothers, 1953).

Bishop Neill's principle calls for the Christian society to be in the world but not entirely of the world. It applies to individual Christians as well as to the Church at large. If men run from the conditions of their environment they cease to be in the world; if they fashion their lives after their environment they lose the distinctive quality that marks Christians. The first error is withdrawal; the second, accommodation. Withdrawal may stress the ultimacy of Christian love but forget its relevance to normal living; accommodation may stress the needs of normal living but obliterate the unique demands of the gospel.

Protestant casuistry must be aware of both the necessity for, and the dangers of, compromise resulting from effective participation in social strategy. It must be guided by a set of principles that will preserve it from opposite dangers. These principles must be understood and applied as a pair. The first is: *A Christian must not withdraw from culture merely to main-*

tain the purity of the Christian ethic. The Christian will participate in the affairs of the world about him even though the
world, in its disobedience and sin, forces him to compromise
the ideal demands of the gospel. But compromise must always
be held in just balance with positive service. Consequently, a
second principle goes with the first one: *A Christian must not
identify himself completely with culture merely for the sake
of effectiveness.* The Christian will not allow himself to become
just another agent of cultural vitalities, content to sanction their
compromises without protest and judgment over them. He will
refuse gross compromise when there is a reasonable alternative
of lesser seriousness. He will prefer not to succeed if the price
of worldly effectiveness is an utter sellout to the pressures of
the world.

Every perfectionistic withdrawal from participation in the
rough business of maintaining earthly institutions violates the
first of these dialectical principles. Monasticism of the Roman
Catholic variety, exclusiveness of the Amish variety, pacifism of
a type concerned only with maintaining an innocent conscience
— all these mistakenly tend to preserve the purity of their life
at the expense of their participation in cultural activity.

Contemporary Protestant thought is full of polemic against
failure to take responsible social action. Most of this polemic
is well taken, but it can be easily overdrawn, as when it accuses
all Christian pacifism of being of the withdrawing type; as
when it sees little distinction between the Quakers and the
Amish; as when it goes so far as to hold that Christians are socially irresponsible if they pursue political activity in an idealistic third party rather than use their influence in one of the
major parties. This polemic, emphasizing the limitations under
which Christians must work in order to be effective in the social process, is preaching the necessity of compromise but forgetting to warn of its dangers. It is just as important that Christians refuse to sanction political activity on its own terms as it

is that they be socially concerned. A second important set of polemics is in order, aimed not at the perfectionists, but at the adaptionists who completely identify Christian duty and secular realism.

Christians must never relegate love to a realm of impracticality and then proceed to deal with society in terms of secular realism. It is not sufficient to work out Christian reasons for dealing with worldly problems in a worldly way. Neither is it sufficient to permit Christian social action to be distinguished from secular social action only by spiritual dimensions of humility and contriteness of spirit, however important these may be. Christians must have more to contribute than a guilty conscience for doing what everybody else is doing.

Ferré maintains that two distinctive dimensions mark Christian activity from the activity of culture. The first is a distinction in motive: the perspective and power of the Christian spring from love. The second is a distinction in action: the Christian will refuse to act when the choices before him are not genuinely constructive, and will rely upon God's ability to act creatively with a power beyond his own. Applying this to the power struggle, Ferré comments:

" Merely to describe the actuality of the power struggle is, therefore, not Christian realism; that is the realism of the world. To describe the actuality of the power struggle with a firm conviction that power belongs to God, and that power can, therefore, be controlled by the Creator in the creatures he has made, is the only Christian realism. Christian realism has for its correct criterion not the description of actual history, but of actual history in light of God's purpose and power " (*op. cit.,* pp. 218 f.; see also the discussion on pp. 133–141).

The role of pragmatic calculation in Christian ethics must always be understood in the context of Christian realism; otherwise it is naturalistic in function if not in name. Sheer calculation, directed by expediency or toward purely humanistic values, is secular and not Christian. Christian obedience can calculate in its service to God — indeed, must do so; yet it ought never to sell out to the secular assumptions that frequently guide social analysis. Christians can never ignore the contributions of the social sciences as a guide in their own analysis, but neither can they uncritically accept all that claims to be autonomous knowledge in the field of social dynamics. Because of different value judgments and world views inexorably bound up with social analysis, social scientists are led to many different conclusions rather than to a single objectively established point of view. There are, for instance, both Marxist and non-Marxist social scientists. For Christians uncritically to accept all social analysis as autonomously valid is as much an error as it is for them to reject its contribution out of hand.

To regard the contributions of technical sociology as the only source of guidance for analyzing the functioning of society is a breach of faith in the significance of the gospel for understanding human life and institutions. Social analysis is usually secular, motivated by assumptions belonging to non-Christian world views. It seeks to be descriptive of society as it actually exists rather than as it ought to exist. Social analysis of this sort may even disallow for the creative possibilities that spring, imponderably, from the freedom of men who are called beyond human bungling into the creative service of God. The genuinely new possibilities created by those called from their normal ways into God's service cannot be predicted or expected on the basis of how society has operated heretofore.

Sin and grace defy reduction to sociological laws. Sociological analysis, even at its best, would likely have missed the creative spontaneity that prompted the early band of Christian followers to break through the bounds of their embodying culture. Sociological analysis in the period of the 1920's, sharing with most secularism the belief in progress characteristic of the era, was not so effective in predicting the rise of modern totalitarianism and the outbreak of a second world war as were a few shrewd prophets who understood the meaning of human sin. While the role of sociological analysis deserves a significant place in Christian thinking, it should not be regarded as the last or final word.

What relationship ought to exist between the proximate strategies and the ultimate principles of Christian ethics? If love that refuses to weigh claims of justice is sentimental, what about justice that turns its back on love? When Brunner bids the Christian operate in the orders of society on the basis of a justice sharply distinct from love, is he giving us the wisest guidance?

These questions cannot be answered except in dialectical terms. There cannot be a complete continuity in kind between ultimate principles and proximate strategies, for this presupposes a more direct relationship between love and the ordering of society than is ever possible in a disobedient world. But, conversely, complete contradictions between ultimate and proximate categories cannot be tolerated, for then love has no expressed relation to social action. Just as we must guard against the pitfalls of trying to apply the ultimates of love to the social order without translation, so we must guard against completely metamorphizing love in the process of translating it into realistic strategy.

The proximate principles of Christian action must not become alternatives or substitutes for love. They must be love's proximate expressions, as proximate to love as they can be at any particular time. Men are called to political realism and concern for justice as an expression of love, not as its substitute. They are not called to political cynicism, to politics as the mere setting of power versus power, nor to the struggle for justice as the mere balancing of competing vitalities in a near stalemate. Criticism of the irrelevancy of most idealistic Christianity must be accompanied by criticism of the unregenerate calculations of the power factions of society. Christians must keep some sense of continuity between love and action, between the ultimate and proximate levels of their ethic. This qualitative continuity is possible because love and culture can meet in casuistry, preventing the divorce of Christian action from the norm of Christian faith.

This qualitative continuity is well illustrated by developments in the area of punitive justice. Loveless justice tends to take the form of controlled social revenge against those who do not abide by the normal standards of society. The fear of punishment is a deterrent to crime; states are justified in extracting penalties from wrongdoers. But enlightened penology sees in its work a much broader task than designing punishment, a task centering about the need to rehabilitate the criminal rather than only to extract a penalty for the crime. This outlook, representing a proximate expression of Christian love, has revolutionized the prison system in America. No fair-minded person would accuse it of having increased crime by virtue of a disregard for the harsh realities of justice.

We must resist the tendency of our age, filled as it is with evidences of man's cruelty to his fellow man, altogether to abandon hope that Christian love can have some expression in the structures of society. To be sure, love is never entirely expressed, but it finds frequent and recurrent situations to which it is pertinent. Such situations will never permit the complete and unambiguous incarnations of Christian love, but they will permit action true to love's basic intent and nature.

When the Christian Church becomes an instrument of social reaction, perpetuating the injustices of a *status quo* by sanctifying them, Christian activity is no longer distinguished from secular activity and the life of the Church becomes coextensive with that of the culture. This creates an obvious and serious corruption in the Church's life. Whenever an evil order is firmly entrenched, the Church ought to break with the powers of reaction and aid the powers that are seeking a new social order. Yet, if, in making an identification of itself with the creative forces of the culture, the Church loses its own specific witness, it will be in no better position. It must be on guard against a tendency to make Christian action coextensive with a liberalism and a radicalism, which, while progressive in flavor, are of themselves just as secular as their reactionary counterparts.

Another dialectic in casuistry, related to the basic tensions already discussed, is the relationship between flexibility and stringency. Casuistry must remember that its provisions are made for man, not man for its provisions. We need laws to serve as general guides to human conduct, but we must not make them into absolute fetishes before which all considerations of special circumstance must bow. If, however, all considerations of law are thrown aside, then casuistry is forfeited in favor of license.

The need for flexibility in casuistry springs from the changes that time produces in human affairs. No strategy, however valid for one period, can be expected to work forever. Religious men in particular must be wary of permitting proximate strategies to hold over beyond a useful lifetime. Not only do new occasions teach new duties, but old occasions vanish away. The Church must be careful not to hold over antiquated strategies and harden them into false absolutes. On the other hand, it is not the business of Christians to champion fads solely on the basis of their novelty. There needs to be some basic relationship between all the strategies that are used by the Church from age to age. This relationship is too often obscure, if not altogether lacking, in the story of the Christian movement. This is not a refutation of the principle, but a commentary upon the inability of the Church to appreciate the continuing implications of Christian love.

One nondialectical principle, however, must overarch the dialectical ones and preserve them from the no man's land of uncertainty. Casuistry will never be Christian except in devotion to Christian love as known in Christ. In the final analysis all Christian action must be justified by appeal to love. Even the compromises of love needed to make it socially real can be sanctioned only by appeal to the compulsions of love and in love's service. Even though casuistry must be flexible enough to deal with concrete and changing situations, it must never forget this stringent element in Christian ethics. Flexibility without stringency is morally weak; stringency without flexibility is harsh and bitter. Christian faith must transcend both relativism and legalism — but transcend them only in ultimate and final devotion to love.

Mere principles of casuistry mean little until they are applied to actual problems, and the theory of casuistry is all too vague until it is applied to a content of casuistry. The structure of casuistry will indeed determine the content of casuistry — but, until the content is discussed and developed, the structure is only theory and its implications abstract. Therefore let us consider the broad outlines of the path along which the Christian should move as he seeks to deal with personal and social moral problems.

PART III

THE CONTENT OF CASUISTRY

CHAPTER IX

The Casuistry of Personal Morality

A WHOLE theological orientation has developed in the Protestant Church of America concerned only for personal morality and content to view the implications of faith in purely individualistic terms. This attitude is common despite the fact that the Old Testament prophets and the writers of the Gospels had a great deal to say about matters of social morality. This ethical individualism, taken as the exclusive concern of Christian ethics, often destroys the social emphasis of the Church. One can overwork the well-known dictum of the Marxists that religion is the opiate of the people, but there is at least a grain of truth in the charge. In the Eastern Orthodoxy of Czarist Russia, in the Roman Catholicism of Europe and South America, in the otherworldliness of some Protestantism in America, religion has so concentrated attention on the rewards of a heavenly bliss as to divert attention away from social questions. Not a few pastors have at some time been subtly approached by members of their congregation with the suggestion that they " preach the gospel " — a request which, being interpreted, usually means, " Say nothing about the social implications of Christianity."

The criticism of religion as a force for social reaction may be overdrawn and its significance greatly exaggerated. Scoffing critics of the Church accuse it of being a rich man's club and of placating the less fortunate members of society almost in the same breath. If, however, the Church serves only the rich, how does it reach the poor in order to placate them with promises of a future bliss? Nevertheless, the criticism cannot be entirely dismissed. Ethical individualism in the Church has been detrimental to the social outlook of some Christians. A shrewd analysis of this problem has been made by *Social Action,* the magazine of the Council for Social Action of the Congregational Christian Churches. This analysis points out how a concern for personal virtues more often marks the interest of the average churchgoer in a candidate for election than does a concern for his basic policy positions. " How a candidate treats his mother becomes for such a voter a better barometer of the politician's competence and worthiness than what he knows or believes about tariffs " (November, 1951, p. 5).

The individualistic morality all too characteristic of religion has cared little for weightier matters of the law, for righteousness and justice in the social order. Its effect has been subtly to undercut the Church's interest in economic and political realms and even to destroy its willingness to challenge unscrupulous exploitation and corrupt political activity. Recognition of this fact and the desire to counteract it has prompted an underemphasis on, and even a distrust of, personal morality among contemporary thinkers interested in social ethics from the religious point of view. To be sure, there is no responsible book in recent Christian ethics that holds personal morality to be unimportant, but the preoccupation of their authors is with the social rather than the personal dimensions of Christian morality.

Moreover, many thinkers have been tempted to oversimplify the problems of personal morality. Accepting the formula " Moral Man and Immoral Society " they have supposed that, while momentous problems of compromise arise in applying Christian standards of conduct to social decisions, the direct expression of love is possible on the level of personal morality. " A man may not be able to act in accord with love serving as a police officer or a judge," runs the argument, " but surely he can do so in his relations to his friends and family."

To disregard the problems of personal morality, or to regard the problems as solved without having to face the problem of compromise, is to leave untouched a basic area of casuistic concern. Personal morality is an important area of Christian living even though overattention to it can make religion escapist. It becomes an area that, in common with all areas of morality, requires the translation of Christian love into practical terms. No matter how much we recognize the necessity of social concern we must be careful not to assume that personal morality has only a peripheral role to play in Christian living. No matter how aware we become of the necessity of compromise in dealing with the relation of love to social problems, we must not suppose that compromise is absent from the area of personal problems. It is necessary that we concern ourselves with the matters of personal Christian morality and, likewise, that we understand that many of the same problems of casuistry and compromise are involved in personal morality as are involved in social and power morality.

Many people define Christian character in terms of a special type of morality. A determined Protestant fundamentalism concentrates much of its attention on getting its members to exhibit a special restraint over the "sins of indulgence." Wheaton College in Illinois, famous as a stronghold of this type of Protestantism, requires "faculty, staff, and students [to] pledge themselves to abstain (*a*) from the use of alcoholic liquors and tobacco, (*b*) from gambling and the possession and use of playing cards, (*c*) from dancing, (*d*) from meetings of secret societies, and (*e*) from attendance at theaters, including the movies." The college regards this rule as founded, not so much on administrative procedure, as on strong conviction about the nature of Christian morality.

This quotation from the catalogue of Wheaton is the extreme, but it explicitly states what many people take as the measure of Christian virtue. Even a widely representative body like the Methodist Church requires of its clergy a pledge to abstain from the use of tobacco. In a great many churches the clergy and ruling laymen still oppose the use of church buildings for social dancing.

Discussion of Christian virtue must be more than a weighing pro and con of these bans on sensate pleasure. It involves the whole question as to the kind of person one ought to be by Christian standards and the kind of person he has to be in order to take his place in the world about him. Seen in this perspective the whole problem takes on a new outlook. The gospel urges men to be humble, to put their trust absolutely in God's care for them, to serve the Kingdom of God without concern for earthly ties, to give their goods to needy neighbors. Some of these admonitions relate to social questions, but they create problems on the individual level as well. Virtue in Western culture is commonly defined in terms of sobriety, thrift, honesty, and success. The world of human affairs judges men far more by externals than by internals. Woe to that man who does not conform to these externals, at least minimally! The Christian faith, however, would measure men by their inner spirit, by their sense of dependence upon God, by their humility, by what in much of the modern world appears as a self-effacement. This contrast moves the casuistry of personal morality into sharp focus. On the one hand there stands the ultimate ethic of service to God, which personal strivings in this world ought not to obstruct. On the other hand there stands the whole complex of society through which men operate in terms of achieved status. On the one hand there is the heroic career-effacing action of an Albert Schweitzer; on the other hand, the sober truth that Schweitzer couldn't be Schweitzer if all men tried to be Schweitzers.

Modern culture creates its most acute problem for personal Christian morality at the point where it demands a concern for the prestige of an external self requiring compromise with internal integrity in order to maintain itself. Many of the demands in a competitive and sensate culture are foreign to the Christian faith. The successful modern man is not the epitome of saintly virtue. This is the point at which the deepest problems arise for the Christian — how to be a working and accepted part of a society whose demands of success are in contrast with the demands of Christian obedience.

The roots of our modern, and now secularized, conception of virtue are partly in Protestant soil. In his Genevan theocracy Calvin insisted that each member of the community render his service to God in a sober, thrifty, and devoted fashion. In contrast to the irresponsibility in personal living characteristic of a medieval Europe in turmoil, the life in Geneva was marked by personal discipline and enforced integrity. This was a casuistic means of service to God by people aware of the need to express this devotion through the action of a sober community. Calvin built a stable community on the basis of dependable individual effort. The life of Geneva was not individualistic in any modern sense, but a rigidly controlled community to which all members bore allegiance as part of their allegiance to God. Calvin provided a doctrine of Christian calling (vocation) that urged men to serve God by devoted industry in their daily pursuits, in contrast to the Roman Catholic doctrine of vocation through monastic effort. This was a casuistry, providing a means of proximate service to God through the normal pursuit of life's otherwise worldly tasks.

It has become popular in some circles to chastise the corruptions to which the Genevan theocracy led, even to blame it for the individualism of modern culture. But only a metamorphosis of the doctrine of Christian vocation turned it into irresponsible individualism. After the period of the Reformation came the great intellectual and social upheavals in Western thought and life which placed man at the center of his own world of values.

These changes in outlook destroyed the religious quality of the Reformation without altering the type of life it created. The sobriety and thrift urged by Calvin as an expression of service to God were transformed into the conceptions of rugged individualism and self-guided destiny that are the mark of the bourgeois movement. A corrupted form of the doctrine of vocation, the original of which was a means of relating one's self to God in worldly pursuits, appeared as the modern idea of self-determination. This idea acknowledges no authority and condones every scheming calculation of personal advantage that doesn't overstep the overt rules of decency. The original conception of devoted individual service to God underlying Calvin's doctrine of vocation has shifted into the idea of worldly success as the measure and mark of virtue.

The Church, not escaping the acids of this process, too often has added to the melancholy spectacle by sanctifying the new attitude as though it were the old one. Worldly success has been taken as the mark of Christian virtue and life " on the right side of the tracks " as proof of obedience to God. The perversion of the doctrine of vocation in the middle-class church is no more apparent than in its tendency to attract intellectual and white-collar workers to the exclusion of manual and industrial workers. This attitude regards mental and clerical work as superior to manual labor. Alas, it forgets that the Lord and Master of the Church was a carpenter!

Sober dedication plays an important place in the casuistry of personal morality. Without it, men flounder about in personal duties and render service to God in careless and slipshod fashion. When, however, men make the idea of individual effort into a goal for its own sake, the goal usurps the place of God and personal effort leads to arrogance in its worst form. Men of strained virtue, seeking their own ends and purposes while trying hard not to appear self-seeking, are colossal boors, poor candidates for the Kingdom of Heaven.

Medieval culture took an attitude toward personal morality that would help to correct and mitigate the emphasis of the modern attitude if only its motivating spirit could be refurbished. The medieval age extolled virtues of humility rather than virtues of achievement. In his list of seven deadly sins, Gregory the Great listed, in order of decreasing seriousness: pride [the source of the remaining six], envy, anger, dejection, avarice, gluttony, and lust. This list of Gregory's is more interesting for its order than for its content. Lust, a sin that might today be regarded as the most blatant, closes the list. Pride, which except in theological ethics is often treated as a virtue, heads it. Gluttony, which in the contemporary world is only a question of health, is a deadly sin according to the attitude of the Middle Ages.

The secularization of this medieval concern for personal humility would result in a " Casper Milquetoast " adjustment to culture, just as the secularization of the concept of self-reliant service to God has resulted in a " Major Hoople " adjustment. Humility is a virtue when connected with devotion to God but is inward and perverted when it lacks such devotion. Self-regard is a virtue when obedient to God in devoted service but is a source of pride and gusto when it lacks such a relationship. Without a sense of dependence upon, and gratitude to, God for all that makes life meaningful and rich, no personal ethic is adequate.

There is a creative interplay here springing from the dialectical character of man's dual relationship — to God and to the culture. To regard ruthless engagement in a harsh and competitive culture as Christian virtue is to sell out to the standards of the world. To withdraw in search of an abject humility is to seek a false perfectionism. In working out a creative tension, such as was at the heart of Calvin's original doctrine of vocation, the Christian will find himself engaged in the very essence of a casuistry.

Now we can return, as indeed we must, to treat the specific problems of conduct usually considered in the field of personal morality. What attitudes ought the Christian to have toward the practices of smoking, drinking, gambling, swearing, and the like? Except in those isolated and protected groupings where such practices are altogether lacking, these are fairly common in our culture. Gambling takes many forms, from betting on horse races at the office to dice games in back alleys. Swearing is particularly a problem for those whose work is manual labor or its supervision. Smoking is so common as to create a problem for anyone who doesn't smoke, and drinking has achieved such widespread acceptance in American society as almost to set off in a minority those who do not drink.

These " petty vices," as they may be called, though not everyone would consider them vices at all, pose a problem for the Christian if his convictions forbid his indulgence. Society has generally come to expect everyone to engage in at least a moderate use of many of these practices. The degree of social pressure for conformity with any one of these practices varies from area to area and from practice to practice. Moderate drinking of alcoholic beverages is, for example, an accepted pattern in Europe among Christians as well as non-Christians. Casuistry must accept these variations, and yet provide for some form of Christian guidance.

Gambling, in the sense of trying to gain money on the basis of chance rather than toil, leads to disruptive results on both the personal and the social level. Men have been known to mortgage homes and starve their families in the effort to overcome losses incurred in gambling. Even the secular order, as evidenced in the laws of most states, acknowledges this corrupting influence. Men resent the enforcement of these laws, however, whenever they are personally prevented from taking part in the games of chance. Most of the laws punish those who conduct gambling and not those who engage in it. The decision of whether or not to gamble is, therefore, a personal one for most individuals. It is easier to resist altogether the temptation to gamble than to stop gambling after one has started. Much can be said in support of a strict refusal to gamble, defended on casuistic rather than arbitrary grounds. Christians can refuse to gamble without compromising any significant social values, but they cannot gamble without becoming party to the disruptive influence of the practice. Gambling has no place in Christian behavior at race tracks, at the stock market, or at the bingo bazaar.

Swearing should be frowned upon in Christian behavior because of the commandment forbidding men to use the name of God in vain. In this sense it has no place in the language of the Christian. The Jews carried this principle so far as to prohibit the pronunciation, for any purpose, of the word "Yahweh," the proper name of the God of Israel. No such extreme rule binds the conscience of Christians; a legitimate use of terms for the Christian Deity has a proper place in worship and theological discourse. For many groups within our culture swear words are the only medium of expression for intense feelings; crude and obscene language has become the mark of worldly toughness. Gang foremen get results with the use of swearing that they do not get with the use of milder language. Christians can help to furnish language equivalents for the impoverished expressions all too common among groups in society where swearing has become the practice. They can never condone impious swearing, nor should they encourage the use of obscene language at club or factory. Again, a casuistic principle rather than a legalistic rule is involved. A healthy " damn " may furnish a verbal outlet for pent-up feelings, and is by no means a deadly sin. When one hits his finger with a hammer he is not required to hold his comment to " What an unfortunate calamity!"

Prohibitions of smoking and drinking originally crept into Christianity in order to prevent the excesses to which these habits lead. The prohibitions were casuistic rather than arbitrary, defended as thumb-rule strategies and not as hard-bound codes. Nowadays the groups that frown on smoking and drinking usually do so on legalistic grounds and exhibit an intolerable and Pharisaical criticism of those who do engage in these habits.

It is desirable to rid Christian ethics of legalistic and crabbed attitudes accompanying these restrictions, but this does not mean to let down all the standards or suggest that Christian faith has no criticism to make of the habits of indulgence. Moderation in the use of intoxicating beverages is certainly the minimal Christian goal, and the Biblical injunction to keep one's body a temple of God can be understood in this light. To let down the bars completely regarding drink is to court the disaster of alcoholism and is ruled out as a Christian alternative. While there is perhaps a greater virtue in the individual who can drink with moderation than in the individual who is censorious of those who do, many can be saved from excess only by a casuistry of abstinence. Abstinence can be the easiest method of preserving moderation and can be justified as a casuistic strategy.

Not a small segment of contemporary Christianity, in justified reaction against the haughty complacency of abstainers and temperance crusaders, has developed a blind spot to the problems created by even moderate drinking. Moderate drinking gives sanction to drinking in general, a major social evil. Social drinking stresses the acceptability of drinking but not necessarily the dangers involved. Men of true distinction do not need the aid of drink to increase their status. The Church can preach with vehemence against all the advertising of our age that would imply the contrary.

The same suggestions apply to smoking, though the dangers of oversmoking are less than those of overdrinking. Many people find it easier not to smoke at all than to smoke in genuine moderation. It certainly is better to smoke than to condemn and rail at those who do, but it may also be better not to smoke than to urge smoking as the *sine qua non* of social *savoir-faire*.

These relatively minor matters serve well to illustrate the tensions in all casuistry. Smoking and drinking in excessive amounts are symptoms of a sensate culture and in the extreme are evidence of its moral and aesthetic disintegration. Refusal to drink and smoke, when prompted by fanatical zeal and self-righteousness becomes the sin of religious pride. The Christian therefore will be on his guard against both those who make an absolute out of refusal and those who make an absolute out of participation in the life of the crowd. He will find himself critical both of Pharisaical self-righteousness in the Church and the uncontrolled use of tobacco and liquor in the culture. The Church must carefully, though firmly, emphasize the dangers in the unbridled cultivation of tobacco and liquor indulgence. If the Church does not sound this warning, few other institutions in our culture will.

A word regarding the matter of social dancing: Here too a prohibition that has hung over from an older casuistry has ended as an arbitrary prejudice against dancing (particularly in church buildings), a prejudice for which few justifying reasons are forthcoming. Surely we have ceased to fear social dancing, though one of the most liberal seminaries in America has only in the past few years permitted an annual dance in its social hall. But are we on guard against the new dangers in this area? Has the formal dance become the normal courting technique for our young people? If so, then we are mating youth under conditions almost bound to sentimentalize and obscure their real personalities. Has the dance become the center of social activity on the campus of high school and college? If so, much in the way of healthy group activity is being forfeited. One of the junior class dances in a well-known American college requires of a person attending it an expenditure of money nearly equal to his room and board for an academic quarter and far in excess of the usual budget which any student church group can raise for the entire year. When social pressure to go to dances becomes so great, one is tempted to advocate, for somewhat different reasons, the casuistry of the Puritans in this area. Dancing must be regarded as a legitimate form of social activity and not allowed to become the pinnacle of social life to the exclusion of all other activities and interests.

The casuistry of personal morality deals with only a limited set of problems. In strictest terms one could say there is no purely personal morality, but that every man must live as unto others. Even a discussion of personal morality involves the relationship of men to fellow men. As the individual takes his place in society the problems of casuistry increase. There is a unique set of problems in the area of group morality, in the area of economic morality, and in the area of power morality. These areas will be considered separately in the succeeding chapters.

CHAPTER X

The Casuistry of Group Morality

BETWEEN the area in which moral decisions involve individual choices of conduct for the self and the area in which men are caught in vast and impersonal forces buffeting them in a web of power relationships there is a realm of group morality with special features of its own. Group relationships may permit a high expression of Christian love, as in the family; they may also bring conflicts of interest and require a special concern for problems of justice, as with the matter of race relations. In fact, the ethics of both sex and race relations fall into the area of group morality. They occupy the attention of this chapter. The development of sex standards, despite the fact that some of the satisfactions of sex accrue to individuals, is a group rather than a personal matter. The achievement of a constructive and just relationship between various ethnic groups, while it requires the use of political power to undercut legal obstructions to brotherhood, requires a level of personal (not individualistic) concern that shows the race problem to be one that will never be solved on the purely power level.

When infused with the ideal of Christian love, with two individuals joined in commitment to each other, sexual experience finds a place among the enriching experiences of man. Permitted to degenerate into animal instinct alone, the sex urge is frustrating and devastating in its effects and it is next to impossible to bring it under meaningful control.

Roman Catholic and other branches of Christendom greatly differ in their attitude toward sex. The Roman Catholic view of sex is essentially negative on both the monastic and the lay level. A dualism runs through the whole Roman Catholic attitude, affirming the somewhat ambivalent norms of monogamous marriage on the one hand and ascetic celibacy on the other. Celibacy is regarded as a higher order of life than marriage and is part of the path to moral perfection in monastic achievement.

The temper of Roman Catholic thought regarding the ethics of sex and marriage is legalistic. The glorification of celibacy is based upon a legalistic use of passages from Paul and the Gospels upholding the idea of celibate living. The attitude toward marriage in Romanism is rigid and fixed, both in its absolutist prohibition of divorce, based on a saying of Christ, and in its attitude toward intercourse, based on a rigid theory of natural law categorically prohibiting birth control.

This legalism develops an essentially negative attitude toward sex. By denying the place of the sex relationship except as the act of procreation it tends to minimize the love-making role of sex. The element of love-making keeps the sex act creative and sacred rather than animalistic. By prohibiting divorce per se, Catholicism evaluates marriage more in terms of cohabitation than in terms of a loving relationship. Refusal to acknowledge the possible legitimacy of divorce tends to put more emphasis upon legal union than upon spiritual oneness.

Protestantism takes love as the guiding principle for sex ethics. This principle saves it from two extremes, the negative legalism of Roman Catholicism and the devastating looseness of modern culture. Sexual intercourse can be sanctioned only within monogamous wedlock and must be an expression of love in order to be human and enriching. It should take place only between two individuals wholly and permanently committed to each other. This clearly rules out all illegitimate relations between the sexes. It rules out arguments for "trial marriages." There is no standard about which there is so little debate within the Christian tradition as the centrality of monogamy to a Christian view of marriage. There is no human relationship more capable of approaching the ideal of Christian love than the relationship of two people in trusting and devoted union with each other.

A stringent rule of monogamy that excludes sexual promiscuity ought to be interpreted judiciously and positively. Negative interpretation of this principle has sometimes made Protestantism as negative toward sex as Romanism. Crass evangelistic preaching about sin has sometimes made sex the symbol of guilt. This negativism was the object of Freud's intense criticism and is the occasion of some contemporary suspicion of religion on the part of psychiatry. We ought to emphasize the Christian standard as a principle of casuistry rather than as a set of authoritarian rules. Christian prohibitions of sexual license are positively directed, designed to protect the growth of love by guarding against practices that would pervert it before it can reach maturity. Youth needs to be preserved in the integrity which ought to proceed consummated union within the bounds of marriage. Prohibitions against sexual promiscuity are not crabbed rules imposed by adults on the flaming enthusiasm of youth, but guides to youth, protecting a higher reward that will come with the institution of marriage. The plea for willingness to wait and to yearn for such a consummation becomes a special burden of Christian teaching in a cultural situation that not only has ceased to cherish these values but has even tended to glorify its scorn of them.

It is easy to suggest that Christians should bear a special burden of responsibility for the kind of preaching and teaching about sex that lifts it into a high and noble context. Guidance as to Christian strategy for changing or reforming cultural conditions that cheapen or commercialize sex is less clear-cut.

Should Christians advocate the legal prohibition of prostitution? Should they seek the censorship of obscene and pornographic literature? Should the Church ban attendance at movies that it regards as questionable and indecent? Ideally, these problems would not arise in a culture that maintained a wholesome attitude toward sex, for the exploiters would not find it profitable to peddle trash. But practically there is much cheapening of sex for perverted purposes and this does a great deal to undercut all the efforts of decent groups to raise the level of the nation's outlook.

Decisions in this area should be guided by the end in view. Self-righteous and publicized bans or openly declared boycotts of movies frequently have the opposite of the desired effect. They increase the spread of interest in the matter rather than submerge it. Behind-the-scenes censorship may avoid this problem, but it runs the danger of curtailing freedom. One is never quite sure when criticism of public media by Church agencies ceases to scan material for decency and begins to limit honest and legitimate criticism of the Church. A Church that seeks to control public morals by political and manipulative techniques rather than by educational and persuasive ones is courting danger. The danger increases as the nature of the morality in question becomes increasingly parochial rather than generally accepted by the common moral code. Bans on movies that criticize special creedal positions are more dangerous to democratic freedom than bans on movies with gross and flagrant disrespect for the minimal codes of decency.

In seeking to rid a community of indecent literature and entertainment concerned groups of Christians can often accomplish much by friendly talk with the proprietors who, sometimes unwittingly, are distributing obscene material. These proprietors may be victims of distribution contracts requiring them to take both good and bad literature from their suppliers. Christians would do well to press for legislation that would preserve for the proprietor the right of discrimination — a right of a free market which in this case is being flouted by the enterprisers. In other situations, as with a house of prostitution, such a friendly strategy would do no good. Here we may be forced to rely on laws either closing the red-light districts altogether or at least preventing them from openly advertising their allurements. It is not a bad rule of thumb in this whole area to insist that each strategy undertake to deal with the problem as simply as possible and use pressure only when other methods prove of no avail.

What is to be the Christian attitude toward the breakup of sex life in cases where marriage proves impossible in the true and the spiritual sense? This question raises one of the knottiest of contemporary problems. Divorce has become a major problem in our culture, and one that can be dealt with only in casuistic terms.

To prohibit divorce, on the basis of either a Scriptural passage or natural reason, is to impose a legalistic and negative attitude on what ought to be a positive matter. The prohibition of divorce must be seen as a casuistic principle designed to emphasize the stability of marriage and to set the atmosphere of permanence within which marital adjustment must take place. Divorce is not a live option for Christian marriage because true and unreserved monogamy is impossible on a take-it-or-leave-it basis. The loose attitude of contemporary culture toward divorce can never become a part of Christian casuistry, for the extent of divorce in our modern culture has become so great as actually to convey the idea of its normality. It is commonly postulated as an " out " if hastily considered, and only half-heartedly consummated marriages do not produce bliss and serenity. The prohibition of divorce is a safeguard against the growth of material irresponsibility. Divorce is a last resort, not a first escape.

In seeking to make laws by which divorce shall be legally

regulated in the State we must remember the purpose of such laws. This is twofold: to undergird marriage with legal responsibility so that divorce is not easily had; to take cognizance of the fact that some marriages are not marriages at all and that legal separation is the only possible escape, however tragic, from intolerable conditions of incompatibility. Some states have laws too loose to do justice to the stability of marriage; others have laws too rigid to accept the tragedy of incompatibility. Christians must be careful to understand that laws of the State are instruments of a practical nature designed to further generally desired ends. They are not the legislation of religious absolutes interpreted legalistically. Pressures by Church bodies seeking to influence the legislation of absolutistic divorce laws are just as dangerous as pressures from other sources seeking to liberalize the laws unduly.

Family life, no less than sexual relationships, should be a channel of shared love. Motherhood expresses outpouring love; fatherhood expresses responsible concern for others. Whatever structure of parental authority is necessary to the ordering of the home must be subservient to the main relationship of love. Discipline will be firm, but it will be present only in a relationship of love that goes beyond the " just " relationship of discipline. Guided firmness prior to crises may do more good than vigorous action once they have arisen.

Faithfulness is important in marriage and family relationships. It is a casuistic principle that helps to maintain the channels through which love operates. Faithfulness may carry family loyalties over the crises that are sure to afflict close and intimate living. In contrast with a culture built too much on the sands of romantic love alone, Christians need a casuistic principle of complete faithfulness, even though they will never regard this principle as a substitute for the true and abiding relationship of love.

Group morality also includes relationships between larger "families" — the ethnic groups which make up society. One of the most important tasks of the Christian today is to relate the principle of brotherhood to means for overcoming the segregated and divided society in which we live. The ultimate principle of Christian love rules out a permanent policy of segregation. A statement adopted by the General Board of the National Council of Churches on June 11, 1952, said this in no uncertain terms:

" Above all, the principle of segregation is a denial of the Christian faith and ethics which stem from the basic premise taught by our Lord that all men are created the children of God. The pattern of segregation is diametrically opposed to what Christians believe about the worth of men, and if we are to be true to our Christian faith we must take our stand against it."

Racial prejudice and segregation, however, are not dissolved by fiat, though prophetic pronouncements and hortatory exhortations have their place, and legal prohibitions of discrimination can force people who otherwise might continue accepted patterns of living to face the issues involved. Casuistry in the elimination of racial discrimination moves between prophetic judgments regarding the brotherhood of man and perverse cultural conditions that violate the principle with flagrant, and often legalized, systems of segregation. The Church is a victim of this cultural pattern, with only about one half of one per cent of the Negro Protestant Christians in the United States worshiping regularly with Christians of another race.

At one time not only segregation, but even slavery, was defended on Scriptural grounds. Perverted teaching of this sort has largely disappeared from the American churches, but the life of the churches still violates the demands of brotherhood. Christian churches are teaching more about racial equality than ever before in their history. The teaching is surprisingly uniform and frontally attacks the whole policy of racial segregation in American life. In fact, some pronouncements in this area are so frontal as to appear perfectionistic, paying little concern to the how and the wherefore of abolishing the segregation patterns in our culture.

When the General Board of the National Council of Churches adopted the statement branding segregation as unchristian, two delegates from the Southern Presbyterian Church offered " a substitute statement which described segregation as an evil similar in nature to ' war, slums, economic injustice, political corruption, divorce, and other unchristian conditions ' " (*The Presbyterian Outlook,* June 30, 1952, p. 5). These two delegates spoke from a situation in which the abolishment of segregation by fiat action might produce social chaos; they were pleading for such transitional caution as would achieve the eventual idea of racial brotherhood without the disruption of other social values.

The amalgamation of racial groups into an unsegregated community presupposes a minimal cultural continuity that would be difficult if not impossible to achieve between two groups as generally different in background and standards as Southern cultured whites and the underprivileged Negroes. The status of the disadvantaged minority has kept them from social and cultural advantages long the property of the whites. There are conscientious people, therefore, who advocate an immediate policy of separate but equal facilities for both races. This policy has as its aim the abolishment of gross inequality between the races and may be advocated as the prerequisite of an unsegregated system. As a casuistic compromise it may have a legitimate place in furthering the conditions, in certain sections of the country, under which two racial groups could in time arrive at true community in an unsegregated society. Too often, however, the doctrine of separate facilities is a ruse, a substitute goal designed to alleviate injustice without achieving brotherhood. When proposed with this motive, it is Pharisaism at its worst. While it is difficult to pass judgment upon men's inner motives, there is reason to suppose that the false rather than the casuistic principle is most often the motive behind the advocacy of equal, but segregated, facilities. The burden of proof lies upon the advocates of such a policy to show otherwise and to explain why, in accordance with the principle of cultural compatibility, inferior whites should not be segregated and superior Negroes accorded all rights of citizenship.

Any casuistry seeking to deal with the problems of racial divisions must be more than a purely personal affair. It is not enough to befriend a man of another race when we meet him personally and then to support a system that legally makes of him a second-class citizen. The overcoming of the evils of racial prejudice and segregation cannot be accomplished by mere individual good will exercised among those who happen to have contact across racial lines. Under systems of segregation such contact is practically prevented. Race problems need to be treated as group problems using social and political means toward a solution, even though these means cannot change animosity to brotherhood in themselves. A group of white and Negro Christians meeting at a church conference must at least be supported in their common friendship by laws that not only permit restaurants to serve them as a group but expect that they will do so.

Patterns of racial segregation are caused by many factors besides difference in cultural status and conditions. They need to be attacked simultaneously on many fronts. Segregated living in New York City is closely connected with economic exploitation, the slum area of Harlem producing more rent per square foot than many of the high-priced apartments on Fifth Avenue. Often it is poor whites, or other minority groups, who are driven to intolerance by fear of competition from the Negro (who often does superior work). These poor classes become the most dogged defenders of segregation and are often the agents of crude mob psychology that works to keep the Negro " in his place." Education of all groups, attacks upon economic malpractices, and Governmental action must go along with any program for the abolishment of segregation. The success of these is dependent upon a minimal ethical support for them on the part of all affected groups. A Fair Employment Practices Act, for example, will work only if there is at least a minimal support for it among the population. Educational and religious institutions have an important function in developing the spiritual climate in which statutory attacks upon segregation and discrimination can carry out their intended roles. This gives an interplay between prophetic pronouncement and political manipulation that is neither the perfectionism of the prophet or the contriving of the politician, but a casuistic middle road that serves Christian purposes amid the ambiguities of culture.

CHAPTER XI

The Casuistry of Economic Morality

A CERTAIN ambivalence marks Biblical references to money and property. On the one hand there are injunctions that admonish men to beware of all riches and to sell their goods and give to the poor. On the other hand there is the command that men shall use their talents in sound investment, and the harsh dictum that those who will not work ought not to eat. Each side of this contrast has, at one time, produced its own type of economic absolutism.

Roman Catholicism has taken poverty to be one of the special gospel counsels and has made it a mark of monasticism — part of the path to perfection for the select few. Protestantism has sometimes produced radical sects that have practiced common ownership of property. Both these practices tend to lay their emphasis upon the Scriptural injunctions to poverty.

On the other hand there are economic practices, not without roots in the Christian tradition, that have sought to absolutize the ideals of hard work and thrift. These have been supported by doctrines of Christian stewardship, lending themselves to the capitalist concept of responsible private initiative. Though their thesis has been qualified by more recent writing, Tawney and Weber have both shown us how this set of values has most often been the guiding principle of economic outlook in the conservative wing of the Reformation Churches.

Ironical notes with regard to both these developments are easy to overlook. Monasticism is very anxious to espouse the ideal of poverty, but once it becomes disciplined the industry and thrift of the monasteries tend to make them among the richest and most landed of institutions. This particular development was most evident in the history of medieval Europe, and it has been mitigated in contemporary times only by careful Church management which channels the riches away from the monastic communities to the service of the whole Church, which holds title to the property involved.

The doctrine of Christian stewardship has a no less ironical development. Advocates of capitalism as a " Christian " type of economic policy are often Biblical literalists, conservative in both religion and economics. The most explicit laws in the Bible regarding economic matters are the prohibitions of taking interest on money lent within one's own religious community. In light of this Scriptural prohibition of usury and the Gospel's distrust of riches it is a bit ironical to find that Biblical literalism should compound itself with economic conservatism. The prohibitions of usury, carried by the Church into the Middle Ages, forced Christians to borrow money from the Jews. The Jews became creditors who were frequently hated and, like Shylock in *The Merchant of Venice,* retaliated with high interest rates because the Christian community was lax in paying debts to " infidels." The prohibition of usury was so strong that it prevented the beginning of modern capitalism until the Catholic casuists of the Renaissance managed to rationalize the spirit of gain, and the energy of Calvinism was secularized so that individual effort was motivated by the spirit of private benefit rather than by the spirit of service to God.

The monastic and sectarian tendencies, both of which seek to take the gospel literally in its teaching about poverty, often end in a false separatism. From time to time Christians have tried to eliminate private property and to establish small communities with common ownership of goods. One of the most thoroughgoing expressions of such an effort was the Digger movement in seventeenth century England — a small group that quickly died out. Legalistic prohibitions of private possessions based upon the gospel warnings about riches often result in utopian communism of a type that does not last very long or prove itself very successful in redressing the inequalities of economic systems.

Idealistic socialism, which shared many of the perfectionistic urges of the sects, was tremendously influential in the era of the 1920's, especially among idealists who thought it a direct translation of the teachings of Jesus regarding economic matters. The evaporation of this idealistic socialism as a political option in our time is largely due to its oversimplification of the problem of controlling (as well as prompting) economic activity in a sinful society where men work only for some degree of self-satisfaction.

In contrast to the perfectionist extreme in monasticism and sectarianism, we find the adaptionist extreme in a secularized version of stewardship. In this corruption of a valid Christian doctrine worldly success is confused with virtue and the accumulation of private property is taken as the mark of personal industry and thrift. The corruption of the doctrine of stewardship into an apology for sensate capitalism is more serious because of the manner in which belief in capitalism has become a political and social idolatry in America. Capitalism is a legitimate and at times highly successful means of organizing the economic life of a community. It has many virtues that men should guard in any economic system. In our culture it has been preserved in a state of health by use of checks and balances that bring its possible excesses under some form of control without basically destroying freedom. But this is not the kind of capitalism about which many of the current slogans purport to speak. Much of the discussion of the values of capitalism is carried on today as though we can be saved only by returning to the days of Adam Smith. All who will not worship the cultural myth of *laissez faire* are in danger of being called "pinks," regardless of how basic is their allegiance to the American democratic system.

Pressures on the Church to make the theory of *laissez faire* the equivalent of Christian truth have been rapidly increasing over the past few years. A great number of the American clergy receive gratis copies of a paper, *Christian Economics,* from an organization called The Christian Freedom Foundation. This paper argues that only a system with an absolute minimum of governmental intervention can be called Christian. It frequently criticizes labor for the use of " unchristian violence " but says little or nothing about the possible coercive power of economic privilege. The free copies of this paper are apparently paid for by lay businessmen who believe, understandably enough, that its editorial policy represents a sound Christian attitude. Spiritual Mobilization, a similar organization with a more sophisticated publication called *Faith and Freedom,* is also active along these lines. It has been organizing conferences across the country for the discussion of economic questions in relation to religious concepts. This group upholds the absolute sacredness of property rights. Other groups with a similar "Old Deal " line are the Committee for Constitutional Government (advocating a twenty-five per cent limit on income tax rates), the National Economic Council, the Foundation for Economic Freedom, and the American Council of Churches. The latter group is an ultrafundamentalist organization headed by a deposed Presbyterian minister who heads a schismatic group of Bible Presbyterians. The organization is largely devoted to attacking the main ecumenical movements of Protestantism, particularly the National Council of Churches, which it accuses of being doctrinally heretical and socially radical. An excellent brief analysis of these groups is available in the May, 1951, issue of *Social Action* magazine, and a fuller treatment is found in a book by Ralph L. Roy, *Apostles of Discord* (The Beacon Press, 1953).

The value of capitalism as an economic order can be affirmed without making it into an idol. Much modern Christianity has been placed in capitalist settings and Christians in these settings must deal with economic issues within this framework. Unless we are to fall victims to the perfectionist error of a sectarianism like that of the Diggers we must work out a casuistry within the constructs of a basically capitalist order. We may seek to amend some features of this order and to mitigate its injustices when they arise, but we cannot dream of utopian economic set-ups that do not exist. There is in sight today no alternative to the democratic capitalism of the free West that even remotely promises to excel it as a workable economic order. Both Republicans and Democrats in America and Tories and Laborites in Britain understand this. The task of Christian strategy, therefore, is to alert itself to the places at which present economic conditions need judgment and amelioration in the name of justice and to foster such strategies as are able to overcome such injustice.

A Christian attitude toward property takes as its starting point God's ultimate Lordship over the whole of life. All human ownership of property is by the grace of God; he alone is the absolute owner. Human ownership of property is never absolute in itself, but is a trust from God, a human right not easily taken away. This has two-edged meaning. It questions the doctrine of absolute property rights currently propounded by some ultraconservative groups; it questions the position held by ultraradical groups that property rights are not important. Property rights can be ignored only under extreme conditions. For any group, even the whole nation, to attach to itself the property of others without payment of due compensation is to flout a stewardship that God has ordained. Where the State needs to exercise the right of eminent domain, it must be allowed to do so only with due process of law and for cases of real necessity dictated by public interest. To propose that the right of eminent domain ought to be categorically rejected because property rights are absolute is to obstruct community endeavor such as the building of highways at reasonable cost in feasible locations. The private individual ought to be paid fair value, but he cannot be allowed to hold up the community for exorbitant compensation. The right of the State to seize property must be exercised only as a last resort and must be hedged by every available legal safeguard for the individual.

If property is a trust from God, then the Christian cannot be content to regard its use as something he may personally exploit without concern for the total life of the community. One of the central teachings of the Old Testament is the teaching about property ownership as a source of responsibility to the community. Those who absolutize property rights in the current ideology of *laissez faire* may recognize this responsibility but they deny to the community any means to enforce it. They readily admit that the individual Christian should exercise his responsibility but forbid the community any recourse against those who use their private property to destroy the welfare of the group. To absolutize *laissez faire* is to make it possible for men to neglect their responsibility to the community in the use of goods and property. When Adam Smith, in a preindustrial and premonopolistic age, first proposed his theory of economics, he was recognizing the quite remarkable fact that reasonable harmony follows the pursuit of personal efforts and interests. But now, when *laissez faire* is propounded as a complete cure for " statism," especially by interests whose immediate pleasures or profits would benefit from lack of public controls, the burden of proof is upon its advocates to show that such a slogan is not a rationalization of self-interest.

A casuistic, rather than an ideological, defense of capitalism serves two contrasting, yet necessary, functions. It provides a basis upon which a particular economic system may be justified; it prevents the confusion of the system with Christianity itself. It is not only unnecessary but also dangerous to suppose that because a particular system is the most promising alternative in the modern world, it is ordained by God for all time and is therefore beyond the reach of legitimate modification. Confusion of capitalism, which is a sound proximate way of ordering economic life, with ideological worship of its tenets is nothing short of idolatry.

Certain middle axioms concerning the creative and positive goals for economic life ought to guide Christian thinking. Economic institutions must be capable of producing sufficient and necessary goods to meet the essential needs of all the people. Failure to meet this test, regardless of how idealistic may be an economic order, will cause its downfall before the performance of more robust, but perhaps less just, means of economic organization.

Equality of opportunity should be provided for men to earn on the basis of their capacity and willingness to work and to receive rewards from the system on the basis of both special effort and their dignity as human beings. Freedom of choice to serve the economic order by contributing constructively to it should be protected. Responsibility rests on society to provide a chance to work and upon the individual to do his work well.

Acquisitiveness and great inequality of wealth must always be kept under Christian judgment. The burden of proof is always upon the privileged to show that their position has not been won by, nor been allowed to become a means of, the exploitation of their fellow men. Unlike Marxist thought, which regards wealth as a priori evidence of vice, and poverty as a priori evidence of innocence and virtue, Christian faith is concerned to make a dialectical judgment upon wealth that fully recognizes its temptations without categorically assuming it to be evil.

Economic institutions should contribute to culture and not determine its character as a whole. They should be compatible with the development of freedom and dignity. The measure of their success should be world-wide rather than purely nationalistic. Christian faith will never accept the achievement of a high standard of living in one country as a blessing if it has been achieved at the expense of, or with disregard for, the conditions in the rest of the world.

Strategy for dealing with economic problems relies upon two main types of control — self-imposed restraints and community coercion. Neither of these is adequate by itself, nor is either satisfactory unless corrected by the other. Conservatives would rely totally upon self-imposed restraints; they assume that an individual sense of honesty toward other business and a benevolent attitude toward employees in one's own business are all that are needed to safeguard the community from the corruptions of great economic power. A paternalistic doctrine of labor relations, for example, leaves it entirely to the management to treat its employees fairly. The employees, if dissatisfied, have no recourse save to appeal for mercy or to quit their jobs.

Self-imposed restraints are important. Surely there is considerable difference between an employer who senses a responsibility for his workers and one who treats labor as " a commodity." No matter what type of system is under discussion one must recognize that self-imposed restraints help to soften its injustices. The absence of a sense of decency and justice in much contemporary economic practice makes for bitterness and cruelty in the industrial and business worlds. Mutual suspicion between different economic groups would be mitigated if more decency and willingness to bargain honestly would be presupposed. Corruption in business, not unlike and seldom less prevalent than corruption in government, would be significantly cut down by refurbishing a sense of personal and group integrity.

But self-imposed restraints are not sufficient, for it is futile to wait for men to do good of their own initiative when they find their self-interest served by doing evil. In a world of disobedience and sin short-run self-interest is served by evil practice. Unless forced to do so by social pressures exerted by the concentrated power of organized labor or the political power of the community, many individuals are unable to understand their part in injustice and even less willing to correct it if they do understand it.

The failure of self-imposed restraints to deal adequately with concentrations of economic power has brought coercive restraints into our present system. One such coercive element is the labor union, which balances the power to bargain collectively against the right to fire at will and set wages by edict. The crucial importance of this development must be understood and protected, especially against all selfish (and even criminal) attempts to prevent it.

The other type of coercive restraint is political. The community has found it necessary to protect itself against exploitation by the unscrupulous, and in many areas the scrupulous have discovered community regulation a blessing rather than a hindrance. In the slogans of our time one would be led to suppose that even such governmental action as setting up a Securities and Exchange Commission and the Pure Food Laws will have to be abolished before we can have a free economy — but there is hardly a responsible group affected by any of these laws that desires their abolition.

Governmental action in other areas is less obviously satisfactory and less widely accepted. Great controversy rages about it. The Old Testament teaching about the responsibility of men to use property for the sake of the community, the control over economic matters exercised by the Church government of the Middle Ages and also by the Reformation Churches, and the insight of Christian faith concerning the necessity of balancing power with power, all run counter to the ideology of *laissez faire.* Luther was a stanch advocate of price control. Rugged individualists had an unhappy time of it in the Geneva of Calvin's day.

The ideological slogans that would abolish governmental activity in the economic field would seem to have little place in a Christian outlook. A great many of the present-day attacks on " statism " would get little sympathy from prophets who judge the rationalization of self-interest after the manner of the Hebrew prophets. On the other hand, Christians ought to be uneasy about the entrance of the Government into economic affairs in any manner that will combine, rather than contrapose, political and economic power. While exponents of a completely unregulated economy are often sentimental about the belief that freedom of all economic activity produces harmony, the exponents of socialistic economy are often equally sentimental in their contention that merely to bring economic process under political control will result in justice. When two vitalities are so joined as to fuse their self-interest, as when political power manipulates economic process, a tyrannical arrogance can easily emerge. Such political action as is brought to bear on the economic process should be regulatory and designed to correct excesses rather than designed to be an economic enterprise in its own right. The advocates of an absolute *laissez faire* will not recognize the legitimacy of governmental control over the economic process; the advocates of doctrinaire socialism usually fail to recognize the need for caution concerning it. The governmental function and the economic system should never be entirely wedded, nor entirely divorced; there must be a give-and-take between these two types of power, lest one of them (or their union) become all-powerful. This may result in a balance of power at the expense of efficiency or harmony, but we shall fail if the give-and-take by which the power of each is checked by the other is lost to an absolutism of either side. The public regulation of private utilities, especially where such companies enjoy a monopoly of services, is a good illustration of this principle. Regulation does not always produce justice, but it prevents the worst forms of injustice and exploitation by balancing political against economic types of power, especially in situations where the normal checks and balances of a competitive market are lacking. Public control of special monopoly must not be ruled out by an ideology that indiscriminately regards all Government interference in the economic process as evil by definition, any more than it should be extended wholesale to areas where major injustices are not present to call for corrective action.

Most Christians do not face these abstract problems except when they vote or discuss politics and economics. The real problems for men come in more practical situations and must be dealt with on this lower level. There is perhaps no cultural pressure that exerts a greater force upon the individual than the necessity of holding a job and of conforming to the accepted conventions of the economic world in order to earn status and advancement.

The temptations that men face in the economic world are not temptations to overt and flagrant dishonesty — this is caught and punished by the business world, as indeed it should be. The temptations that put the Christian conscience in the agonized position of compromise are those which arise out of the tendency of modern business to lay a total and all-demanding claim upon an individual — not just upon his skills and services during office hours. He is expected to dress according to certain standards, to live in the right section of the suburbs, to drive a particular type of automobile, to stay at the office late at night or work at home without regard for his family, and to move at the will of the company, irrespective of the effect of such a move upon domestic life or the psychological and educational adjustment of his children. The price of nonconformity to these demands is lack of advancement and the possible loss of job. These pressures are especially acute among the class of people who attend the "respectable" American churches.

An individual seeking to buck this pressure is almost helpless as long as he must earn his living in this type of work. Change of jobs does not alter the situation unless one changes his work altogether and deliberately decides to pursue personal and family values that cannot be replaced by money, nor had amid the bustling drive for large financial returns. Success is not measured by the five-figure column if along with it go broken family ties and a mad scramble to climb the ladder of promotions at any cost to self-enjoyment and attention to the finer things of life.

Surely Christians cannot all run to a fire-tower watching post (as did one family, which thereby found a great new and enriching life without any of the conveniences of modern living). They can, however, cut down on their endless drive for more income if this drive is self-impelled and not necessary to the holding of their job. They can also challenge the pressures of our world which are driving thousands, particularly in the junior executive class, in the relentless scramble for external and monetary success. Against this madness the Church can certainly raise no less protest than has *Fortune* magazine in studies during recent years. The Church can do more than merely criticize. It can point out to men the satisfactions possible without high incomes and the enduring values of life on which no price tag can be placed. It can also console and comfort and heal men caught in this web of circumstance from which they cannot immediately escape. Whatever else Christians do, they must never accept with a complacent conscience the drive for material success that marks our age or cease to look for the opportunity to break its rigid claim over men's lives.

To deal with economic problems in the larger context involves many facets of power morality, as the main considerations of this chapter indicate. Politics and economics are intertwined, as even those who use politics to keep politics out of economics know full well. It takes political action to control political phenomena, even to curb political power from absolutizing itself into a totalitarianism of either a Fascist or a Communist type. Therefore, in assuming that political power has some relevance to economic power we raise a new set of issues. These issues concern the relation of the Christian to the world of power and the casuistic strategy that he must employ in seeking to bend its purposes to the service, however partial, of Christian ends.

CHAPTER **XII**

The Casuistry of Power Morality

How, if at all, should Christians participate in politics? Should they become active in ward clubs, city organizations, machine party politics? How are they to make a choice between the platforms of various parties and the personalities of various candidates? If Christians are loyal workers in a party, can they exercise a Christian judgment over it?

How, moreover, should Christians deal with the problem of participation in violent coercion designed to preserve justice? Should they, or should they not, participate in warfare, and if so, on what grounds? How can Christians deal with the compromises of Christian love, even the contradictions of love, that are found in the coercive features of society?

Problems of power morality pose the sharpest difficulties for the Christian conscience, but they are sooner or later encountered by all Christians, either consciously or by default. The world of power is a realm of harsh reality, often at variance with the ideal of Christian love. Participation in politics, and particularly participation in warfare, poses sharp problems for any ethic of decency and especially for the Christian ethic of love. Much political action and most all forms of violent coercion are difficult to reconcile with the nature of love. Withdrawal from participation in these realms, however, leaves the world at the mercy of forces that do not hesitate to exploit it for their sinister purposes.

One of the widespread tendencies in modern thought is to make little or no distinction between the nature of political action and the nature of participation in war. Colloquial reference sometimes dubs both " dirty business." It cannot be denied that the sanction of political power is often military, or at least pseudomilitary, and, conversely, that military power is coagulated only around centers of political organization. Nevertheless, significant and crucial distinctions mark political action apart from participation in war. To equate the two realms, as though to hide the distinctions between political process and military strategy, is to becloud the issue. Some of the problems in both areas can be treated together, but our discussion will need to return to the matter of their delineation.

Two extreme positions regarding power morality are easy to recognize and may be rejected on the part of a Christian casuistry. The perfectionistic extreme is represented by a type of moralistic objection to the compromises involved in power conflict that prompts withdrawal from it. The adaptionist extreme is represented by the uncritical participation in power decisions that completely identifies Christian faith with partisan and jingoistic programs.

Withdrawal from politics is often based upon pseudoaesthetic motives. Politics requires the making of common cause with groups whose conduct and cultural habits are sometimes crude and rough. It may also require moral compromise. It may be necessary for Christians, for example, to make common cause with a party machine that protects forms of organized vice in order to secure proper educational facilities in a city. In other situations it may be necessary, in order to support a move for clean government, for Christians to support a party that will seriously impair the city's welfare services. It is seldom possible to choose a political party whose platform represents all the right positions or to reject a party without also rejecting some positions that one would like to see advanced. In sober moments all people will agree at this point, regardless of how they may talk just prior to an election. A political party is not a group of sterling knights on a crusade, but a loose amalgamation of various groups many of which are seeking to serve their self-interest. To withdraw from the " mess " because one hates to be identified with it is to leave the determination of political decisions to those least anxious to make them for the common good.

Withdrawal from participation in warfare is usually a quite different matter. There is an aesthetic non-Christian pacifism that hates war because it is an unpleasant business, but this is only of minor significance. This aesthetic pacifism lacks the moral stamina required to carry through a conscientious objection to war and is not recognized by the draft laws as legitimate grounds for exemption from combat. Christian pacifism, however, is prompted by deep and powerful adherence to the Christian ideal of love. The pacifist may oversimplify the task of relating love to the problems of justice in a coercive situation, but this is a critique of his strategy and not of his motives. In fact, a Christian cannot really have thought through the implications of Christian love unless he has at least been tempted, and allows himself to be continually tempted, by the pacifist case — even if in his final agonized decision he may not follow it. No criticism of Christian pacifism, or its failure to deal with the harsh reality of power, should obscure the fact that its motivation is fundamentally based upon a deep-seated devotion to the ideal of Christian love.

The literature of Christian ethics during the past fifteen years is full of polemic against withdrawal from both political and military struggles for power. This polemic came as a much-needed stimulus to the Church to study more closely the relationship of Christian love to power decisions. It has made the Church aware that power is a relentless and inescapable factor in the formulation of policy and social structure and that refusal to deal with power on a responsible level disregards the very process by which mankind can be preserved from tyranny and corruption.

But the polemical attack upon the perfectionist error has tended to decrease sensitivity to the adaptionist error, the error of urging Christians to participate in struggles for power without also warning against the dangers involved. It is the error of saying that Christians must accept the necessity of using and balancing power in accordance with wise, though almost altogether secular, calculations of necessity. The adaptionist error is most apparent, not in sophisticated and sensitive thought, but in a secularized Church that does not separate the demands of patriotic zeal from its version of Christian virtue. The customary intolerance of pacifist thought in the parish church, the identification of Christian goals with absolutized victories in war, and the almost complete failure of Christian groups effectively to qualify the actions of their respective nation-states, all form the pattern of adaption.

The casuistry of power morality is marked by two poles; the absence of either breaks the necessary tensions between Christian faith and political concern. Reinhold Niebuhr puts it thus:

" The test of a creative relation between our religious life and our political action is a double one. On the one hand the question is whether the life of faith prompts us to participate responsibly in the struggle for greater justice. The other question is whether our faith prompts us to discriminate, rather than indiscriminate, partisanship " (editorial in *Christianity and Society,* Autumn, 1951, p. 5).

Discriminate judgment over political activity means more than mere argument for participation in such activity. Christian faith must go farther in its relation to political affairs than simply to urge participation in political struggle. It must go even farther than to urge participation in the proper side of the struggle. The relationship of Christians to political decision is doomed if the Christian ethic is totally compromised in order to deal with the harsh realities of political necessity. A major function of Christian faith with respect to political activity is to transcend the partisanship of a conflict, not by idealistically refusing to make common cause with a particular side, but by refusing to identify completely the interest of any side with the will of God or *the* Christian way. We must be as fully aware of the dangers of militarism as we are of pacifism, and just as critical of the tendency to military absolutism as we are of pacifist idealism. Military power per se does not make for responsible action; Christian faith can never condone the jingoistic glorification of military action and heroism.

Many sensitive Christians have a line at which they will no longer sanction conflict. A few will not participate in any military action; others will ask for medical service in the armed forces. Still others will participate in combat but seek to guide the policy of the nation into constructive channels and away from the false glorification of war. During the last war the Calhoun Commission was constituted to write a report: *The Relation of the Church to the War in the Light of the Christian Faith*. After the bombing of Japan with nuclear weapons it issued a supplementary report, *Atomic Warfare and the Christian Faith,* in which it condemned the indiscriminate atomic bombing of Japan. This report was frequently criticized, undoubtedly because it came closer to criticizing national war policy than any other official Church statement in a great many years. It is an example of the Christian judgment over war that must always be made. No Christian dares finally to equate the cause of his own group with final righteousness. There ought to be a recognizable distinction, as there is in all the courses of action outlined in this paragraph, between the conduct of the Christian in a power struggle and the behavior of the culture.

Christian casuistry in the realm of power morality will never be complacent regarding the outcome of power struggles in which proximate issues of justice are at stake. Too often Christian idealism, in crying, "A plague o' both your houses," in a conflict, gets soft and muddleheaded in this regard. The Christian will make discriminate judgments between contending vitalities in conflict; he will be concerned for the preservation of that side in a conflict which most nearly serves the cause of justice and truth. But he will always point out, however unpopular it may be to do so, that no one side in a conflict ever monopolizes righteousness.

An element of critical judgment over the action of the group is necessary to a Christian casuistry. While such a judgment is difficult to maintain except on a theoretical level, it is an exceedingly important element. Our cultural power groupings are rapidly destroying the restraints over power that make civilization possible, as they push to ever more furious forms of totalitarian warfare. At least the ancients had rules for the game, but modern nations seek the utter destruction of their adversaries. Christian faith can never sanction this tendency, and ought to be hypersensitive to the misuse and overuse of all power at a time when the cultural tendency is to be callous and absolutistic in the manipulation of force. The Christian is never permitted an easy conscience in the struggle against evil. The secular zealot can fight in self-righteous arrogance in a " holy " crusade, but the Christian will constantly press for reconciliation as his ethic of love prompts him to dynamic, outpoured, and unceasing effort to transcend struggle with reconciliation and love.

Christians will engage in reconciling work amid all controversy and remain determined that political struggle shall not destroy a chance of reconciliation. Effectively upheld, this principle would set the Church in considerable opposition to the policies of modern nation-states. Now, the Church is too often an agency that stamps approval on the policy of its culture or simply cries in the wilderness without affecting decisions of policy at all.

Struggle can never be the ultimate nature of political action, for truly creative political action involves constitutional achievements of peaceful order in the community. This factor separates the area of politics from the problem of war. The building of constitutional justice into the political order must be a perennial concern of the Christian who is seeking to make love relevant to society. The achievement of justice is not the automatic result of success in conflict. It is the hard-won outgrowth of a creative process that involves the creative interplay of human resource working in harmony rather than conflict. Christian attitudes toward conflict, however grudgingly they may admit the necessity of power, must be careful to emphasize the place of creative justice in the whole political order. The Christian will be concerned about social unrest and injustice prior to the advent of full-scale conflict. The usual attitude toward war tends to elicit the highest degree of concern and sacrifice once war has begun and to condone quietism (e.g., isolationism) only prior to an outbreak of hostilities. A culture has pseudopacifist tendencies during times of peace (unless it is tempted to some form of power imperialism) and a jingo war ethic in times of conflict. A Christian might almost be advised to reverse this — to foster every type of peaceful coercion and concern needed to eliminate trouble spots before they enlarge into full-scale conflicts and to seek throughout the conflicts to restrain the passionate war ethic of self-defense so as almost to qualify the interests of the nation-state.

In the situation of cold war, which is a type of power struggle that has broken in upon our generation, the culture is tempted two ways at once. It is tempted to isolationism on the one hand, to pretentious use of its power on the other. Christian faith will steer away from both, utilizing its insights regarding the responsible use of power to prevent isolationism and its insights regarding the dangers of power to prevent imperialism in a new guise.

Restraint over power must be prompted by prophetic rather than merely prudential considerations, for the purely calculative use of power is never sufficiently sensitive to the dangers of its own excesses. In this regard strong pacifist sentiment, which has all but evaporated from most of the Church, may have unique political significance. The issue between pacifism and nonpacifism must always be a dynamic one, for the tendency of pacifism is to be perfectionistic and the tendency of nonpacifism is to be adaptionist. It is not a good omen that as warfare gets increasingly violent and unreserved the pacifist voice in the Christian Church should become increasingly weaker. Pacifism has little chance of being adopted by the culture as its strategy, but it can furnish a needed corrective that keeps cultural policy from blowing itself up with an uncritical use of power.

There are many levels of power struggle besides the military. None of these levels avoids the dichotomy between itself and the claims of love, but some of them are more creative than any future suicidal form of warfare can ever hope to be. Strategies of nonviolent resistance and non-co operation may have limited place in power conflicts. They certainly cannot be considered free from the ambiguities of power manipulation in general, but neither can they be ruled out as legitimate alternatives to the utter futility that would probably come from modern unrestrained war. Too often pacifists have presented such strategies as the Christian way to deal with threats of power, forgetting their ambiguous nature. Equally often the nonpacifists have refused even to consider such strategies as a possible expression of Christian action.

It is not always easy to translate these abstract and dialectical considerations into practical decisions. A youth perplexed about going into service needs another form of guidance. A Christian counselor should point out to a troubled youth the significance of his troubled conscience. Such a troubled conscience is evidence that at a personal level the real issue has basically been faced. The counselor will suggest that the troubled conscience cannot be escaped by a Christian whose loyalty to Christ and to the standards of Christian love is always in tension with an unfettered loyalty to cultural standards.

With this perspective fruitful discussion can proceed to practical decisions. It is important to understand in all such discussion the ambiguous character of the possible alternatives, both the values they preserve and the values they negate. There are three basic Christian alternatives: " conscientious participation," as Richard Niebuhr has called it; conscientious objection to combat types of military service; conscientious objection to all military service. None of these escapes the problem of compromise. None ought to be undertaken with a complacency of conscience that does not agonize over the inadequacy of its own decision. No Christian can say that it is his duty to serve the nation proudly and without qualms of conscience, nor can he say that a Christian who refuses to fight escapes all the compromise. He must always understand the agonized tension between the demands of the nation and the ultimate demands of love.

There is no area of greater perplexity than this area of Christian casuistry. The Church will do well to seek a more common mind on these matters, but also to beware of the oversimplifications that could characterize a common mind at which it too hastily arrived. Perhaps we shall never altogether solve the dilemma posed by power for the Christian conscience and shall always agonize over the problem. If this be true, then we arrive at the limits of casuistry. We may be able to define the extremes to be avoided but never to come to an altogether satisfactory ethical decision. The youth with a troubled conscience adds a new and very important dimension to the situation of the Christian. He knows the limits of his own power and virtue. The Christian teacher must never destroy such sensitivity, for it is the very transitional experience by which ethical concern leads into redemptive faith.

This is not antinomianism, saying that it makes no difference how men decide the issues. It is not legalism, saying that they ought to decide them one particular way. It is a recognition that even the best of human guidance demands faith, demands a " beyond casuistry " in which God's grace alone can make men whole. Only by understanding this truth about all ethics and all casuistry can we be true to the heart of Christian faith.

BEYOND CASUISTRY

CHAPTER XIII

The Limits and Dangers of Casuistry

CASUISTRY can be justified only as an instrument by which we relate Christian love to the ethical problems that daily face us. Casuistry is a tool in the service of love, but it is always in danger of claiming to be more than a tool. It frequently attaches to itself the claim of a divinely sanctioned code and develops into a legalism of hard and fast rules. Then casuistry ceases to deal with the necessities of individual needs and clamps men into a rigid mold from which there is little escape. Religion always surrounds itself with the aura of sanctity, and this entrenches its perverse as well as its valid features. The principles necessary in the development of casuistry are not always kept in the role of proximate principles. They become confused with the primary loyalties of which they ought to be only the expression. When this happens, casuistry ceases to be casuistic in the true sense and becomes a system of codes substituted for Christian love.

Hardened and perverted casuistry is as old as casuistry itself. The provisions of the Deuteronomic Code, at first casuistic provisions designed to keep Israel faithful to the religion of its covenant with God, hardened into religious absolutes. In the rabbinic teaching of Pharisaism, commentary on the law, designed to ease the law in light of special circumstance, turned into new law. The rabbis, dealing with a typical problem of circumstance, treated it thus:

" If, said the law, a person was murdered on the highway and the assassin was not discovered, the nearest town must bring a calf as an atonement. If, however, the corpse was found halfway between two towns, where on the dead body should the measurement begin to determine which town must bring the calf? Rabbi Eliezer said one must measure from the navel, but Rabbi Akiba, with elaborate reasons based on man's creation in the image of God, argued that one must measure from the nose " (H. E. Fosdick, *op. cit.,* p. 116).

A provision such as this is actually a casuistic interpretation of a casuistic principle. It would no doubt call for another interpretation if the body happened to be lying exactly midway between the towns crosswise of the road! As arguments about such trivialities proceed without end, the main ethical principle is forgotten. The towns forget their responsibility for justice and order and the protection of travelers. The second-order casuistry in the illustration and the third-order casuistry that might prove necessary to implement it in a special case are less valid than the casuistry of the first order. The original casuistry is an attempt to measure specific circumstance against ultimate principles; its reworking obscures the principles altogether.

As long as a casuistry is aware of the ultimate standard that it seeks to implement it is likely to be valid. When it degenerates into the manipulation of minor matter versus minor matter it becomes both absurd and perverse. It multiplies specific formulas in an endless attempt to care for every special type of every special case. Only by measuring each decision by the intent of the original standard can sanity be restored to such a system. One of the limits of casuistry is the incapacity to preserve a valid relationship to the demands of Christian love save as each decision is re-examined in fresh awareness of those demands.

If code moralities, as Paul Ramsey calls these legalisms, only appeared outside of Christianity, our problem would be simple. But Christianity produces legalistic rules out of the perversions of its own freedom, particularly by hardening its own valid casuistries. Roman Catholicism and sectarianism, which place a heavy emphasis upon the ethical side of religious faith, most readily produce code moralities.

Roman Catholic moral theology bases much of its guidance upon appeal to rational criteria. Thomas Aquinas, by holding that the reason could determine standards of natural virtue apart from faith, introduced into Catholic thought a system of rules that men can supposedly verify on reasonable grounds. Roman Catholic thought prohibits all birth control on the rational ground that sexual activity is meant for procreation. It determines a " just " from an " unjust " war on the basis of five (mainly outmoded) criteria. It has a categorical answer to the question of mercy killing, an answer regarded as legitimately binding on both the secular and the religious order.

The Roman Catholic scheme tends to inflexibility and supposes that its criterion of reason can be accepted by all men, both within and without the Church. Catholics assume that there are some eternally binding standards even apart from the special standard of Christian love. Paul Tillich calls this attitude a " static supranaturalistic " approach to the relation of ethics and historical change. He describes it as follows:

" With tremendous psychological power the static supranaturalistic solution maintains the eternal and immovable character of the ethical norms and commands. Philosophy and theology co-operate in this direction. The world is conceived as a system of eternal structures, preformed in the divine mind, which are substance and essence of everything and which establish the norms and laws for man's personal and social practice. Philosophy discovers these structures and laws, revelation confirms and amends them. And revelation adds some superstructures of its own that are new and higher laws but equally eternal and immovable " (*The Protestant Era,* p. 151. The University of Chicago Press, 1948).

Fixed and binding laws founded on human reason apart from Christian love require a casuistry that is other than a casuistry of love. If these moral laws are categorically true for the ordinary level of conduct, then hard-fixed rules can be postulated for all the varying conditions that are encountered in their application. These rules are not attempts to implement the demands of Christian love, but are elaborations of the principle of reason. Thus, like the casuistries of the second and third orders which have ceased to be casuistries of love, they have lost their true home.

Protestantism also formulates rules of behavior that have lost their relationship to Christian love. Whenever casuistry is formulated by appealing to the literalistic meaning of isolated Scriptural passages, the Protestant equivalent of code morality is apt to appear. Paul Ramsey cites the case of a " sect of Russian Mennonites [that] frowns more on smoking than on drinking, on Scriptural grounds, since Jesus said not what goeth into a man, but what cometh out, defiles " (*op. cit.,* p. 47). Literalism of this type fails to relate its specific standards back to the ultimate standard of Christian love. Even in cases where the exegesis is sounder than in this illustration, casuistries founded on a proof-text method are prone to woodenness.

Many of the codes surviving in the Church today have been taken over from our Puritan forefathers without the accompanying reasons for which they were first worked out. Many of the Puritan codes had a sound casuistic justification, but this justification has been almost entirely forgotten. Casuistic rules become legalistic codes unless their validity in new circumstances can be established by appeal to the principle of Christian love. They cannot be safely transmitted from one generation to another except as the reasons for their development are also transmitted and revindicated. Just as casuistry grows legalistic when, in the case of second- and third-order considerations, it forgets the demands of love, so also it grows narrow when its rules are transmitted to second and third generations of Christians without the transmission of the understanding that relates these rules to their original intent.

Casuistry loses sight of its relationship to Christian love, not only by becoming legalistic, but also by becoming too flexible and accommodating to the standards of the world. Casuistry is the process of relating the demands of Christian obedience to historical necessity. It is tempted, not only to claim too much for its strategies, but to claim too little for its ultimates and to identify its proximates with a secular way of doing things. Christians, easily overcome by the disobedience of the world with which they seek to deal, forget their ultimate allegiance to love in order to be thoroughly realistic and relevant to the world. They cease to bring to bear upon actual ethical choices the prophetic criticism demanded in both theory and practice by the perspective of faith. This perversion, opposite to the perversion of legalism, is akin to what Tillich calls the "dynamic naturalist" solution to the problem of relating ethics to historical change.

Whereas the legalism of Israel expressed itself in the stringent laws of Deuteronomy, the disobedience of Israel expressed itself in its desire, at the cost of diluted faith in its own God, to make common cause with the nations about it. The attempt of Israel to make its life secure in the flux of its eastern Mediterranean corridor by courting the favor of other nations in political alliance was not a cynical or corrupt disobedience. It was an effort to secure definite and tangible benefits from political policy and careful diplomacy. But the prophets denounced it as apostasy, as a worldliness that issued in secular strategy and destroyed faith. The prophets were more concerned about syncretism in Israel's relation to its cultural surrounding than about legalism in its own ethic. The preaching of many of the prophets contains an absolute condemnation of Israel's attempts to preserve its national existence by barter and diplomacy rather than by faith in Yahweh, its God.

> "My people have committed two evils:
>   they have forsaken me,
>   the fountain of living waters,

and hewed out cisterns for themselves,
broken cisterns,
that can hold no water "
(Jer. 2:13, R.S.V.).

Men of faith are always tempted to conform to secular pressures and to the mores of expediency. Casuistry adds to this temptation. Christians can easily see apostasy and unfaithfulness as manifested in the world of secular affairs, but they can less easily see and admit the situations in which the community of faith has itself been secularized. The Church is tempted, as was Israel, to secure its life by letting secular pressures go unchallenged. The established and conservative Church in all traditions can become secularized because of its dependence upon temporal security. Groups that hold the content of their teaching to purely doctrinal matters concerning individual salvation can rob faith of its prophetic criticism of conditions in the world about it. Sects that regard their teaching as binding only within the community of faith can forget their responsibility to the world at large. In any case the Church ceases to be a transforming leaven in the social order and its casuistry fails to do its proper work. Without a casuistry Christianity cannot relate itself to secular orders; with a loose or a false casuistry it may equate itself with them.

The dangers of casuistry are opposite in many ways, yet they evidence the same fundamental failure to be ultimately loyal to the demands of Christian love. Legalism, which develops when casuistic principles and codes become ends in themselves, can appear only when love has been made subservient to the rules for its application. It can be broken in its strangle hold over a religious system only when the demands of love are given fresh and bold restatement as in the teaching of Jesus. Apostasy, which develops when casuistry leads into a complete identity between religious and pagan strategy, is likewise a failure to be faithful to love. Apostasy can be broken only by a recalling of the religious community to its primary loyalty, as in prophetic preaching of God's absolute claims on human life.

It is easy to define the dangers to which casuistry is prone, but how can the dialectic be maintained by which legalism and apostasy are avoided? How can the dangers of casuistry be prevented from gaining the upper hand and spoiling its valid function? These are the problems that stand at the very heart of faith and take us into the area beyond casuistry.

Casuistry does not help men to preserve its own most fruitful expression or to correct its own excess. The greatest limitation of casuistry is an inability to be self-purifying. It is only safe as an expression of a devotion that goes beyond it. Men do not strive to serve Christ in the world about them except as some power from beyond them prompts their service. If they undertake that service for the sole benefit of self, they will pervert it. If they undertake that service forgetful of its temptations, they will confuse their own limited accomplishment with the will of God and grow fanatical. There is no safeguard against religious fanaticism save the sensitivity given through the Holy Spirit, by which alone fanaticism can be detected and judged. Men are not humble by virtue of their own power to destroy self-centeredness.

Casuistry must be undertaken in the framework of faithful reliance upon God. It must be chastised and corrected by a power beyond itself. This power must keep ethical devotion true to Christian love and recall men when they stray from allegiance to it. To argue this way makes little sense to the advocates of a non-Christian ethic. It makes little sense to the pragmatists and humanists who, having no resources beyond their own strategies for dealing with human problems, are forced to rely upon the self-sufficiency of their ethic and the self-correctiveness of its equivalent to casuistry. Whereas the secularist, who believes in no power beyond that of human skill and wisdom, must calculate and scheme with only human resource, the Christian may work as in devotion to God. This devotion may include calculation but can never be reduced to it alone.

The casuist must recheck each ethical decision against the norm of love and not merely judge it by its practical fruits or short-range results. To this end he must know the master plan. A man who builds a house must cut and fit each individual piece, but if he does so without checking the whole building against the larger guides of square and plumb line, the building will be lopsided and out of true. Likewise, the cutting and fitting process of casuistry will build properly only when checked against the standards of the gospel.

The gospel ethic never lets us go; it calls for a continual striving after a goal that admittedly will never of itself be attained. We hear much these days from the theologians about the scandal of the gospel in the metaphysical realm, but there is also a scandal in the ethical realm. It is the demand for a total abandon to the unconditional claim of love in order that its conditional claims may be properly managed. An element of intense ethical devotion that lies beyond casuistry is the only power that can preserve casuistry from its errors.

Casuistry can be a noble service to God only when it is an outgrowth of a devoted faith which lies beyond it. The process of dealing with life on the level of normal necessity is the daily task of the Christian. This task can be undertaken safely only as an expression of absolute loyalty to God's will. This loyalty can be spoken of only in prophetic terms. A minority may sense this prophetic demand for all of life, but most Christians have prophetic insight for only a few areas at a time. They must bear the burden of keeping one another loyal to the whole gospel through mutual aid and correction. Prophetic absolutism does not furnish strategy, but it is relevant to strategy in that it seeks the ultimate perspective by which that strategy can alone be judged. It challenges the disobedience of society by preaching the demands of total obedience.

But important as this radical preaching of the ethical demand may be for the purifying of casuistry and for the health of the Church, it does not bear the final word. The final word by which men are saved comes from God in his justification of men by faith. This word emphasizes that men are saved by God's own power and love and not by casuistry or ethical devotion, however strong and valid they may be. Beyond casuistry there is both an ethic that corrects casuistry and a faith that saves ethics.

CHAPTER XIV

Ethics Beyond Casuistry

CASUISTRY is a valid process only when it is related to love's ultimate claim and seeks to serve that claim. Casuistry cannot, however, keep alive devotion to love's demands and cannot correct its own failures to be loyal to love's demands upon the Christian conscience. Religious faith dies unless this loyalty is kept alive, unless there is maintained in the conscience of believers a burning devotion to the ethical ideals of the Christian faith. Conditional strategies in casuistry can be safely pursued only as a means of service to the unconditional requirements of faith. It is this unconditionalism alone that is able to break the legalism of code morality and also to recall men to Christian living when they have sold out to secular pressures.

The unconditional and absolute demands of Christian love find expression in two types of ethical outlook. The first type is ecstatic ethical devotion that, in scorn of consequence, pursues the knowledge of God's holy will in utter dedication to it. The second type of outlook is the prophetic temper, preaching the absolute character of God's requirements with little concern for circumstance. To say that either of these, or both together, furnishes the only necessary element in Christian living would be to reject the whole casuistic process; to deny them a necessary place would be to destroy the very standing ground from which valid casuistry springs. Ecstatic devotion and prophetic absolutism are not substitutes for casuistry, but mentors by which it may be kept from error. To systematize the role they play in ethical decision would be to reduce them to the level of casuistry. They can be understood only as ethical phenomena beyond casuistry by which casuistry may be kept in a state of spiritual health.

Ecstatic devotion perceives the absoluteness of God's demands and strains to meet them. It may turn into frenzied zeal unless checked, but without its presence in casuistry the service to God that is intended through compromise action turns into a scheming of men for their own selfish interest. Ecstatic devotion is needed to preserve a sense of unreserved loyalty to Christ. The pressure of culture is toward complete compromise. This complete compromise is not only an inadequacy of ethical service, choosing the lesser evil, but a wandering from the service of God through any channels. It threatens to reduce casuistry to sheer pragmatism and to destroy the claims of Christ upon the believer. Only when this pressure of culture is countered by the dynamic of religious devotion can men be kept aware of the demands of Christian love.

Prophetic absolutism, which is always coupled to ecstatic devotion, declares that God alone is ruler over men's lives. It challenges the false rule of any casuistry that takes its strategies too seriously. It is usually by prophetic preaching that men are jolted from their cherished idols and disobedient ways. Furthermore, prophetic absolutism is the channel through which the ultimate demands of Christian love are revealed to men and kept before human consciousness.

Casuistry, in seeking to wrestle with the needs of men, tends to lose sight of the absolute demand of love. Casuistry has never been, and will never be, an instrument of the revelation of the nature of love. The Old Testament prophets were not casuists but devoted advocates of an absolute ethical obedience. They speak to our condition with more pointed meaning and insight than do the casuistic writings of the Pentateuch. To interpret the prophets of Israel as advocates of sensible and reasonable political strategy is to miss their message. Amos predicted a nearly complete doom of Israel because of its moral laxness; Hosea pleaded for a return of Israel from the strategy of syncretism to absolute, and primarily religious, devotion and trust in the Lord; Jeremiah was the counterpart of the modern pacifist, content to see Judah become the victim of an ethically inferior Babylonia. As champions of politically realistic strategy the prophets are poor statesmen; their message is meant for another dimension, calling for an unqualified conception of obedience to God.

Likewise, the teachings of Jesus are beyond the realm of casuistry. They are not concerned to lay down strategy for immediate historical decisions. They are concerned about the absolute level of Christian love and the unconditional duties of man to God the Father. They judge and criticize the casuistry of Pharisaism, so hardened in its codes as to pervert its own best insights. Jesus seemed little interested in the pressing political problem of his day, the Roman conquest and plunder of Palestine. Surely he knew its horrors and injustice. His refusal to sanction revolt against Rome was not dictated by expediency; expediency never ruled the career of Jesus, especially in his steadfast decision to go to Jerusalem. His refusal to lead the Zealots cannot be taken as a guide to social strategy for all time, as some political pacifists would take it, for this would make it into a binding example that would forever tie the hands of Christians from throwing off injustice. Not a strategist, but a prophet, Jesus was concerned for religious judgments rather than historical successes. Thus he revealed God's absolute nature and will.

The cross on which Jesus died is also an example of utter abandon to the demands of faith marked by ecstatic devotion. In the cross devotion to an ideal passes beyond the considerations of political success. There has been much fruitless debate about the relation of the cross to social strategy. Some thinkers have regarded it as the very example of suffering love which ought to be the guide for Christian action. Reinhold Niebuhr, on the other hand, warns that it cannot be turned into a success story. The cross defies reduction to casuistic strategy, but it still has great ethical significance. " True love ends up on a cross," according to a well-worn saying — but in so doing it reveals the nature of true love, and when the cross is that of Jesus Christ, it sets the whole framework of Christian loyalty.

We can be thankful that Christ's teachings are not detailed prescriptions. We should be glad that Jesus was not a casuist. The temptations to legalism would be irresistible, had Christ laid down a code for men to follow. As in Mohammedanism, where followers imitate the prophet even to minute details of daily living, any religious system that uses a casuistry as its final means of teaching its ethical standards ends up in code morality. As they stand, the life and teachings of Jesus will correct all casuistries that function in his name whenever these casuistries depart from service to his cause.

Devotion to Christ is the ecstatic element in Christian ethics. It is the appeal of Christ as the Master of men that makes them serve God in faithful obedience. The contemporary Church needs a rebirth of devotion to Christ. This ought to be one of its most distinctive marks, but it has been lost on the practical level, with the Church's identification with the world, and on the theological level as well, where talk of devotion to Christ is sometimes criticized as a sentimental hangover from liberalism. The most pressing problem for any ethic is the problem of motivation. Faithful obedience to Christ as Lord is the source of the Christian's motivation. A zeal to do God's will (even using casuistry as a tool in the process) is not prompted except by the infusing of the community of faith with a new spirit of devotion and obedience to Christ. Nels Ferré, flaying many of the most prominent Christian theologians of our day for their failure to acknowledge and exploit this truth, insists that the

Christian acts in the distinctive dimension of the Holy Spirit. The action of the Christian in the Holy Spirit, according to Ferré, is expected to result in constructive dynamic achievement. " Whatever be the exact combination of texts and their finer meanings in the New Testament," he writes, " there can be no question about the fact that the New Testament means us to have radically changed lives by the powerful presence of the Holy Spirit " (*op. cit.*, p. 137).

Men do not die for great causes on the basis of casuistry; they do not enter great adventures while participating in ambiguous decisions with a sense of humility. They become fired with passionate obedience to God only when personally confronted by Christ. The formula that was taught many of us in our youth, " Do what Jesus would have you do," may have led to simple formulas for the solution of human ills, but it fired us as its present-day substitutes no longer are able to do. The contemporary Christian movement needs to find a dynamic interplay between ecstatic devotion to Christ and a sober, critical, and realistic means of implementing it. Casuistry in the true sense may be able to meet this need.

In having to keep all its strategies under the rule of Christ the contemporary Church is not unlike the historical Church. Ecstatic devotion has always been a crucial factor in maintaining the dynamic quality of Christian living. By the creative sacrificial lives of the saints and martyrs the faith of the Church has been preserved through social conditions that would have snuffed it out or adapted it to pagan codes. This level of ethical devotion produces heroic action, and the Church is blessed by the heritage of men who have maintained it. By such devotion the continuing awareness of the Church can be held sensitive to fresh and dynamic implications of Christian love for the ongoing process of history. Christian love has been completely revealed in Christ, but we can never do without new prophets to relate its truth to our present age. Concern that Christian ethics be realistic and practical and politically responsible must never be allowed to deny a place for the prophet.

Whenever the Church has opposed change with a social conservatism springing out of a casuistic concern for the preservation of positive values in an existing social order, it has been challenged by a radicalism of love in sectarian movements. The place of radical sectarianism in the Christian tradition must be understood as the place of the prophetic absolutists. Sectarianism is not a simple or perfect alternative to the conservative life of the organized and established Churches. Of itself, it usually advocates a politically unrealistic policy. Sectarian Christianity is devoted to a radical type of living which stirs the Church itself from lethargy and the misuse of casuistry. The Christian movement is better for its presence.

Radical sectarianism can correct and chastise the casuistry of the Church as a whole even though it can never be turned into a simple alternative to that casuistry. The practical relevance of radical love ought never to be underestimated. All casuistry tends to conserve the values of a given social order rather than to risk an alternative and untried set of substitutes; radical love can correct this when it needs correction. All casuistry tends to calculate with excessive concern for self-interest; the radicalism of love can correct this. Too much casuistry tends to make its pragmatic judgments on the basis of secular analysis coming from world views that are only peripheral to the Christian faith; the radicalism of love can correct this. All casuistry tends to assume that the outcome of social policy is dependent entirely upon human action rather than divine providence; the radicalism of love can correct this. Through these corrective influences the radicalism of love has practical relevance to casuistry, helping to correct it and keep it true to its main loyalty. Enlightened self-interest is never sufficiently enlightened for its final self-interest (which is to serve God by giving of itself rather than seeking to preserve itself). Human wisdom is never sufficiently wise to understand that what men regard as desirable may not be what God regards as permissible. Men are as frequently destroyed by the folly of their own wisdom as by the excesses of their religious zeal. Ecstatic devotion can serve the politically relevant function of awakening men to the folly of their accepted ways and spurring them to change and amend them.

In order to be valid, the content of any intense ethical devotion must be Christian. One need only observe the pseudo-religious fury of Russian Communism to be made aware of the possible evils that spring from devoted zeal when it is divorced from humility and a sense of judgment under God. But to note the deluded self-righteousness of such secular extremes is no reason for excluding from the Christian experience a legitimate place for ethical absolutism as a corrective factor in the life of the Church. Every movement in history that breaks established patterns is motivated by a zeal that transcends casuistry and its concern for established values. The Christian may refuse participation in choices that completely lack a creative relationship to faith. Like Luther, in his break with the Roman system, finally able to propound new truth only within new structure, the ethical prophet will at times reach the place where his only words can be, " Here I stand."

Within the freedom of this ecstatic devotion to love, Christians can act when the normal codes of behavior cease to have any real guidance for them. The action demanded of members of resistance movements in totalitarian countries may be undertaken in this freedom. Out of this freedom Christians will act in times and conditions when the assured outcome is altogether questionable and their action is a leap of faith. Casuistry will work much of the time, but it is well to know when it ceases to work and to be able to transcend it. Casuistry can be transcended safely only when its possibilities have been fully exhausted, and only by appeal to the norm of love of which casuistry is meant as the proximate expression.

This cannot be made into a vindication of absolutism in all the proximate issues of life. The extreme situation cannot be read back into the normal ones in a way that replaces casuistry with frenzied zeal. But neither can the extreme situation be forgotten, nor its special needs denied. Christian action must not be entirely limited to the casuistry that preserves established values, else it will dilute the creative possibilities of God's continuing word for the affairs of a contemporary day.

All absolutism is open to dangers. Even the ethical accomplishments of prophets do not create flawless social harmony. No human action is the incarnation of full Christian love. Men are tempted to fanaticism if they do not understand this fact and govern their attitude accordingly. The love of Christ passes judgment over all human actions. Men are preserved humble by the recognition of this truth. Even ecstatic ethics cannot be a means of salvation. The ecstatic level of ethics often disrupts social order for the sake of a new order, and the wounds inflicted by this process can be healed only by a power beyond the range of ethics. The redemptive function of faith is beyond ethics, and therefore beyond casuistry — though in the power of God it not only transcends both but becomes a redemptive part of them.

CHAPTER XV

Faith Beyond Ethics

I T IS difficult for men to accept the doctrine that they cannot save themselves through moral works. Especially is this true of those who adhere to a highly ethical religion like Christianity. To follow the ethical ideals of Christianity, its casuistry included, can lead to a pride in virtue that corrupts even saints. Just as casuistry cannot correct its own faults, but must be corrected by an ethical devotion beyond casuistic concern, so ethical good works do not bring salvation except when they are coupled to faith in a higher power that can make ethics meaningful. There is a realm of faith beyond ethics, even as there is a level of ethics above casuistry. This realm of faith does not cancel the need for ethical devotion, nor deny its subordinate significance, but completes the meaning of ethical devotion and furnishes the ground out of which ethical works ought to spring and through which they become meaningful.

The Roman Catholic Church has not always understood this truth as profoundly as it might and places too much emphasis upon the role of works in the process of salvation. It makes ethical and sacramental works essential aspects of salvation. Catholics are admonished to work in rigorous ethical devotion, in hopes that they may fulfill the law. Monasticism provides the zealous few a chance to strive endlessly for the attainment of the goal of perfect obedience. The casuistry of such a system becomes a precise definition of ethically permissible works; a careful guide to right action in every specific situation of uncertainty, a science of maintaining the validity of one's own good works and of avoiding transgression of the law.

Casuistry in the Catholic sense also has come to mean guide rules by which penance is assigned by the priest-confessor. Men who have transgressed the law, consciously or by default, may confess their sin and perform special works of grace and penance by which they can again earn acceptance in the community of faith and in the sight of God. Holding, as it does, to the view that men must fulfill their duty to God through ethical works, Roman Catholic theology is forced to provide a set of penitential works through the performance of which men may atone for their previous failings. This is to attempt to cure breaches of the law by further use of law. As a scheme by which men may supposedly earn their reacceptance by God following a wrong act it has no place in Protestant thought.

Protestantism holds that salvation is assured to men on the basis of their faith rather than of their works. Sometimes committing an error opposite to that of the Roman Catholic Church, it has placed the ethical side of religion in a secondary and unimportant role. On the "Billy Sunday" level it may manifest an evangelistic concern so exclusively occupied with right faith as to forget the ethical reorientation of the convert. On a responsible level it may become exclusively concerned with the content of dogma rather than the quality of life expected of Christians. Sensitive Protestantism will guard against this perverted neglect of ethics, even though it puts final trust in the role of faith. Christian obedience ought to be an expression of ethically concerned faith. Faith is the primary but not the exclusive category. Men who shun all responsibility for their works do not have true faith. Faith is not license to ignore the demands of ethical duty. The primacy of faith in Protestantism is not set over and against works as though to destroy their significance. Rather, faith is set above works in order that they may be fruitful in the sight of God.

God does not measure men by their output of virtue. He measures them in love by their willingness to trust his goodness and to acknowledge their need of his grace. Even the most conscientious of men will fall short of God's holy will. The very need for, and reality of, a Protestant casuistry makes this clear. Men of faith who fall short of God's demands, especially when they acknowledge their inability to serve God perfectly, are still to be found in the love of God.

Faith does not play the role of mopping up the debris left by human failure to do good works. The redemptive activity of God is a profound mystery not to be caricatured in this fashion. It does accept men even though they are unworthy according to the law of ethics, but it also relates to their own understanding of the function of ethical devotion within religious faith. When men believe that they must justify themselves by works, their casuistry hardens into a set of rules defining the letter rather than the spirit of the law. When, however, men believe that they will be justified by grace through faith, then their casuistry can be a devoted abandon, doing all that it can to relate Christian love to a world in which its full and absolute expression is not possible.

Protestant casuistry is the strategy of the devoted Christian seeking to live and to work in a disobedient world. The believer seeking to be obedient to Christ will always acknowledge his own temptations to disobedience. Thus he will be helped, by God's grace, to resist these temptations. He will acknowledge his inadequacy for the task laid upon him, and thus be the more adequate. Those who engage in casuistry with a conscience that is sensitive to the contrast between the demands of Christian love and their own service of love cannot but know the need for divine grace. Knowing their need they will experience its benefits. Casuistry is a service to God amid the ambiguities of human life; it brings no permanently satisfying results from its ethical accomplishments. It becomes meaningful in the satisfying sense only when transcended by a faith that can assert that the compromise is accepted by God as a reasonable service. Such a faith boldly believes that God loves man in spite of his sin.

A casuistry that operates in this perspective will not be tempted to become a legalistic substitute for faith. As men see their human service against the far higher demands of God's will, they will be forced to acknowledge their dependence upon God's love. They will not seek the precise rules of action found in a legalistic code, but will strive to the utmost of their limited ability to do the works of love in a sinful world in accord with a casuistry of love. They will serve God, as the Bible suggests, "with fear and trembling," leaving room for unlimited ethical devotion even though such devotion can promise only limited success. The primary struggle of the Protestant soul is to avoid the type of complete compromise with the world that would utterly destroy its relationship of obedience to God. The struggle is the very essence of Christian faithfulness. It is a soul-taxing process.

Even when men succeed in the struggle to remain faithful to God, it is their faith, and not their ethical works, that justifies them. Casuistic choice is between ethical grays, compromises, and ambiguous alternatives. God accepts choices made within this pattern as the reasonable sacrifice of faith. His redemptive power, not the virtue and cleverness of human works, heals the breach between human effort and divine demands. This radical denial of human self-sufficiency, which may at first appear to destroy ethics, actually re-creates it on a fruitful plane. It frees the Christian for a creative response to God by enabling him to operate as a man of faith amid the ambiguous choices found in all human existence.

To understand and acknowledge both the theory and the experience of this truth is the first step in repentance. A Protestant conception of casuistry actually moves toward repentance because it freely acknowledges the necessity of compromise. In casuistry undertaken in this perspective men become aware that they make choices in a world of imperfect and difficult alternatives. Within this perspective men will see the need of repentance and their inability perfectly to fulfill the demands of obedience to Christ.

If men can explain away the claims of Christ by holding themselves responsible only for what they can accomplish through ethical good works, they will feel no need of repentance. If they deny the ultimacy of ethical standards by acquiescing in the philosophical secularisms of our age they will even deny the validity of repentance. But if the demand upon men is so high that they can never be ethically perfect in the sight of God, then they will acknowledge the possibility of being saved only by casting themselves on his forgiving mercy. If the ethical demand can be satisfied by works, then men can hope to save themselves by ethical, including casuistic, effort. If the law is irrelevant, then men can excuse themselves from its demands and will need no casuistry. But if the law is both ultimate and relevant, then faith is demanded and alone can resolve the predicament of man.

Casuistry, and even life itself, is meaningless and futile unless justification by grace through faith is presupposed. Life always involves compromises. These can be undertaken in the knowledge that God will accept faithful human service, however partial, and redeem it by his power. Apart from such a belief only despair can afflict the human soul. Despair may take the form of desperately trying to perfect one's life by conformity to an ethical ideal. It can take the form of altogether giving up to the disobedience of the world. In either case it has ceased to be an obedient service to God.

Justification by faith does not destroy the place of duty. Men must both implore forgiveness on their knees and rise to work. The work can be done in the context of forgiveness and is best done when it is not regarded as a path to salvation earned by its efforts. Moral striving leads to despair when fulfillment of the law is attempted, yet a worse despair has already set in if ethical concern is not evident at all. Faithfulness is obedience to God; it implies ethical service of the casuistic type. Faith presupposes obedience and obedience must be undertaken in faith. Justification by faith can never mean release from the ethical demands of God in so far as it is within the capacity of men to fulfill them.

The power of God working through his Holy Spirit in the obedient soul not only forgives sin but furnishes a power of new life that carries the believer into a new relationship to God. Without such a power casuistry is not the faithful compromise of obedience seeking to be relevant to the world, but the fruitless disobedience of compromise with the world. Only through a moral transformation effected by God can men change the basic orientation of their lives. The Lordship of Christ is not a call to slavish following of minute laws of conduct, but unreserved commitment to Christ as Lord and Master of human life.

"The Biblical idea of justification not only offers us the right understanding of the meaning, scope, and goal of moral standards; it also provides an effective motive for right action and the strength to do good. In his life of faith the believer embraces the purpose of Christ who wants to transform this world into his Kingdom, and he does so out of love and gratitude for what Christ has done for him, not merely because it is morally or practically necessary to do so. Thus Christian ethics pursues a divine rather than a cosmic or humanistic goal, and its motivation is purely religious" (Otto A. Piper, "Justification and Christian Ethics" in *Theology Today,* July, 1951, p. 176).

We ought to be bold and unashamed at this point. Our casuistry is not a theoretical adjustment of the ultimate to the proximate but a service to the divine Lord and Master in a world that dishonors his way even when it bows to his name. The meaning of Christian experience is found in the relationship of obedience as undertaken in response to the forgiving love that has been made known to us in Christ. Without the love of Christ to ennoble and redeem it the whole enterprise of Christian ethics is frustrating.

The last word of the gospel does not concern the ambiguity of ethical choice but proclaims God's grace in Christ. The gospel promises a redemption that comes despite compromise. Sensitive men are all too aware of the tragic and compromising nature of historical choice, of the contrast between Christian ideals and historical actualities. For them the gospel comes as promise — a promise of God's acceptance through faith of the best that they can do in the face of this difficult contrast. Casuistry is a necessary strategy, sin presupposed, for relating God's ultimate demands upon us to the condition of a sinful world. It can therefore make no sense unless the good news of the gospel goes beyond it. Casuistry is made necessary by the fact of sin, but it must help men to creative action beyond that sin. There is no more pressing need in the present hour than for a Church of Christ that can use casuistry in order to bring to a disobedient society the creative energies of the Christian spirit.

In the seventh book of *The Republic,* Plato tells the story of human beings chained in a cave, able to see only their own shadows cast by a fire against a screen. They mistake the shadows for reality. Outside the cave there is the light of the sun. The prisoners in the cave cannot easily look at the light of the sun because their eyes become blinded by its brilliance, and consequently they content themselves with the shadows of the cave.

The modern Church lives in a secular world. Largely unaware of its condition, it becomes a prisoner in a cave that hides the light of God. It fails to see the light of the gospel because it is preoccupied with the shadows of the cultural conditions it mistakes for reality. Much of the Church actually resists, by expelling its prophets or ignoring their preaching, the light of the gospel as it judges human institutions — institutions cherished by men because they can see no other hope. Christians should seek so to change the Church, and subsequently the world, as to let God's light shine into the darkness.

Christians will uplift the world with a casuistry in its real and proper sense. Casuistry must never be a process that enables Christians to adjust to the darkness of the world. It must never be a process by which Christians escape from the darkness only to leave their fellow men behind. The light that can shine into the world shines of its own power, a power initiated in the grace of God. It is for Christians to seek to conquer the sin that keeps out the light. They will overcome evil only as they understand the true depth of their own darkness and the false nature of the shadows that they, in company with all other men, are always tempted to take for reality. Men may not like the light, but in faith, by God's grace, they may be given power to look upon the light despite the holden character of their eyes.

Men will never become the source of the light. The gospel does not promise that they shall overcome the darkness of their souls with their own illumination. It does not even suggest that men will seek to get out of darkness by their own initiative. But it does promise that when men remove the sin that separates their own life from the light of God, then God's light will shine in.

Faith demands performance of a reasonable service to God to the full extent of human capacity. The creative possibilities of human life when devoted to God must never be underestimated, even though faithful men are forced to compromise because other men make no effort to follow God's calling. There is a continual tension between the divine will and human accomplishment. Men are called to serve God within the historical conditions of this tension — to serve God within the conditions of life that surround them. Even so, they must understand that their best service is only partial and that they must throw themselves on the mercy of God. If men cease to seek the best that they know, their repentance is a sham and their casuistry a spurious avoidance of duty. But if men do the best that they can by means of a casuistry that seeks to relate the demands of Christian love to the actualities of life, recognizing the finiteness and compromise involved, then for them the gospel has truly good news, the news of the gift of grace in Christ by means of which alone men are made whole, and the life that they live is transformed into an acceptable service of God.